VIVA MEXICO!

VIVA MEXICO!

CHARLES MACOMB FLANDRAU

A traveller's account of life in Mexico

WITH A NEW PREFACE BY
NICHOLAS SHAKESPEARE

ELAND BOOKS

Published by
ELAND BOOKS
53 Eland Road London SW11 5JX

First published in 1908 by
D. Appleton & Co, New York

ISBN 0 907871 20 8
First issued in this paperback edition 1982

Printed in Great Britain by
Redwood Burn Limited, Trowbridge, Wiltshire and
bound by Pegasus Bookbinding, Melksham, Wiltshire,

Cover Design © Philip Wills
Cover Photograph © Mansell Collection
Map © Patrick Leeson

TO

DON GUILLERMO

OF THE FINCA DE SANTA MARGARITA

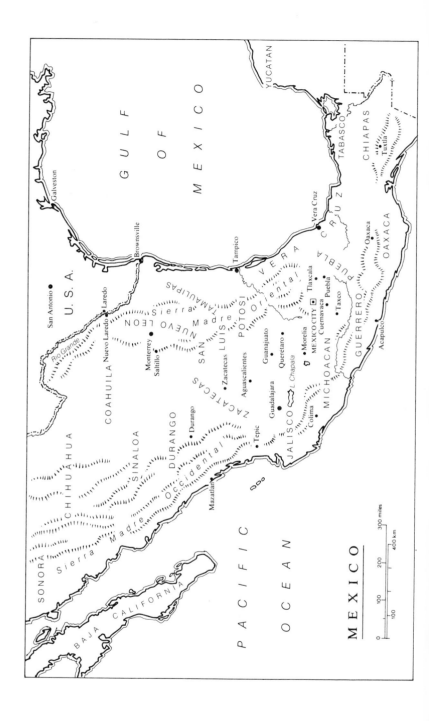

MEXICO

NEW PREFACE

'To be a god is to be quite detached from all around, or else so permeated with everything as to be part of it.'
R. B. Cunninghame Graham—*Mariano Gonzalez*

'Mrs. Grill is very ill
And nothing will improve her
Unless she sees the Tuileries
And waddles down the Louvre.'

So quoted Trollope in his *Travelling Sketches* of 1866, as an example of the assumption that travel is an ameliorative occupation, and that home-staying youths have ever homely wits. It was an assumption he challenged. His first sketch depicts the family that goes abroad 'because it is the thing to do.' Father, mother and daughters cross the Continent because it has become socially imperative to see an Alp and drink German beer. Their only gratification is to finish the voyage. 'At last they are home, the penance is over and the true pleasure begins'—in the recounting of adventures. Trollope's man who travels alone, someone called Robinson, has embarked on his tour with much compunction, dreading his solitude and believing in his heart of hearts that it would be better to accompany his sisters to Broadstairs. He latches on to Jones, the first man he meets, who, having asked the poor fellow which way he meant to travel on the morrow 'had plainly told him that he and his party intended to take another route.' As Trollope adds, most of us are Robinsons. He cites other types: the art tourist who 'looks for his return in that sort of reputation which is now attached to the knowledge of the history of painting.' The Alpine Club man who, having inhaled the air, keeps his nose in it, 'with a conscious divinity of which he is . . . not quite able to divest himself.' And the unprotected female tourist, a middle-aged, fastidiously-dressed woman always to be met with on the Nile.

The Victorian in Trollope's sketches believes, like Allan Quartermain, he had attained 'the highest rank that a man can reach on this earth.' When he sets foot in foreign fields, he sees himself as a god detached from all around. He is a tourist, by and large, who enjoys having travelled, but who, as Flandreau later observes, rarely enjoys travelling. Having taken his own world with him, he lives cocooned within it, becoming even more bonded to his prejudices. Lady Florence Dixie crosses Paragonia with her terrier and tinned *asperges en jus,* and returns realising only how important is 'the tittle-tattle and small talk of ordinary life.'

Trollope's most notable omission concerns the traveller who is so permeated with everything as to be part of it. Charles Macomb Flandrau is one of these. His *Viva Mexico!* was written on the eve of the Mexican Revolution, and the transition from Diazpotism (as he calls Porfirio Diaz's ruthless regime) to democracy. It has, with some justification, been labelled one of the best travel books ever written.

Flandrau was born on December 9th, 1871 in St. Paul, Minnesota. The son of a lawyer-historian— who had acted as an agent for the Sioux indians—he first developed a taste for travel when taken to Europe at the age of eight. At Harvard, he combined a democratic outlook with a basic irreverence that found an outlet in *Harvard Episodes* and *The Diary of a Freshman.* In 1903, an inheritance from his father allowed him to replace undergraduate themes with his earlier love of globe-trotting. For five years he made repeated visits to his brother's coffee planta-tion in eastern Mexico; he toured Russia, France and Finland, and after working for a time as a critic and columnist in St. Paul, he sallied forth to Africa.

Thereafter, until his death in 1938, he divided his life between America and Bizy in France—the original home of his Huguenot ancestors. A well-to-do bachelor with a hankering for privacy, his public offerings were comparatively few—a handful of collected sketches with titles like *Prejudices* and *Loquacities*. None were to eclipse his earliest travel book, *Viva Mexico!*, first published in 1908.

Viva Mexico! has been out of print for many years, but even today it is not out of date. Flandrau carried no pre-conceptions with him, and finding a land where theory and practice were so far apart, he dispensed with guide-books. Mexicans, he discovered, 'have a genius for stringing words upon a flashing chain of shrugs and smiles—of presenting you with a verbal rosary which later you find yourself unable to tell.' In Mexico, *no hay reglas fijas*. There are no fixed rules. Personal experience became the chart by which he steered, and by depending on it he was able to fathom the Mexican's mongrel temperament even more completely than Lawrence and Huxley after him; his passion for both seclusion and publicity, his yearning for colour and movement, his superstitions and his violence. No place is out of the way for Flandrau. Everything is unique, Mexico City resembling absolutely nothing in the world except itself.

To such an extent does he conceive of the country as 'one long, carelessly written but absorbing romance', that his chapter on the Trawnbeighs was included in a fiction anthology. What is mistaken for invention is, in fact, idiosyncratic emphasis.

In the capital's theatres its was said that the prompter had to read everyone's parts. In *Viva Mexico!*, Flandrau sits tranquilly on a bench in the plaza and does the same with those who pass by. Recalling Archduke Maximilian, who tried to become Emperor of Mexico, he looks up at the balcony windows where the impenetrable ex-patriates bluff their way through life; people like the Trawnbeighs who usher guests into the 'north wing'—a bamboo shed, dressed in ball-gowns that look like poisonous wall-paper. Though they have lived abroad for fifteen years, they know no Spanish, and remain exactly as they would have been had they never seen the place. Next door is a smart hotel, advertising the delights of American home-cooking, where Trollope's tourists are putting their Kodaks to bed and Mrs. Grill is complaining loudly that she wouldn't trust any of these people with a cent.

'The most notable sight in Mexico,' though, 'is Mexico itself.' Flandrau's real enjoyment comes in recording the semi-private existence of the world and his wife promenading down one side of the square and up the other. He sees a policeman kill a drunken shoemaker. A Bishop with a fat overhanging lip gravitates towards the Cathedral, and through the trees the coffee-pickers struggle home under the weight of their baskets.

Flandrau is Lord of all, 'the only one really intelligent foreigner in the republic.' Just as his brother is able to wrest the secret of drinking-coffee from the little berries, so he peels the tough red outer skin from this fascinating, mysterious country, and serves us with something that has retained its flavour for over seventy years.

VIVA MEXICO!

I

NEITHER tourists nor persons of fashion seem to have discovered that the trip by water from New York to Vera Cruz is both interesting and agreeable. But perhaps to tourists and persons of fashion it wouldn't be. For, although the former enjoy having traveled, they rarely enjoy traveling, and the travels of the latter would be pointless, as a rule, if they failed to involve the constant hope of social activity and its occasional fulfillment. By tourists I mean — and without disparagement of at least their preference— persons who prefer to visit a country in bands of from fifteen to five hundred rather than in a manner less expeditionary; and persons of fashion I am able even more accurately to define to my own satisfaction by saying they are the kind of persons to whom the wives of American ambassadors in Europe are polite. Probably to neither of these globe-trotting but alien classes would the voyage from

New York to Vera Cruz appeal. For the tourist it is too slow and long. There are whole days when there is nothing for the man in charge of him to expound through his megaphone; whole days when there is nothing to do but contemplate a cloudless sky and a semitropical sea. Thoroughly to delight in the protracted contemplation of such spacious blueness overhead and of so much placid green water underneath, one must be either very lazy or very contemplative. Tourists, of course, are neither, and while persons of fashion are sometimes both, they are given to contemplating the beauties of nature from points of vantage favorable also to the contemplation of one another.

Emphatically the deck of a Ward line steamer is not one of these. A preliminary investigation just before the ship sails rarely results in the discovery of what a certain type of American classifies as " nice people." When nice people take sea voyages they usually go to Europe; and so there is an additional anticipatory thrill on embarking for Mexico in the certainty that there won't be any merely nice people on board. The ship will be crowded—so crowded, in fact, that at Havana and Progreso (which is the port of Merida in the Mexican State of Yucatan) the company's agents will distractedly swoop down on you and try to convince you that it is to your everlasting advantage to abandon a lower berth in the stateroom long experience has enabled you to select, for an upper berth in a room you happen to know is small, hot, and near the steerage. If you are amiable you laugh at them, but if, as is customary, you and the company have had a fierce disgusto before sailing and you are therefore not amiable, you express yourself without restraint and then run to the rail to watch the agents depart in their launch, with gestures that more literally resemble the traditional tearing of hair, wringing of hands, and rending of garments than any you have yet observed.

The ships are crowded, but not with the kind of people who set sail in search of pleasure, or the Beyreuth festival, or health, or the London season, or clothes, or the Kiel regatta, or merely because they are temporarily hard up and have to economize for a time by dismissing the servants, closing all three houses, and living very simply in nine ballrooms at Claridge's or the Ritz. With people bound for Latin America, Fate somehow seems more actively occupied, on more intimate, more intrusive terms than it is with people on the way to somewhere else. Most of them are going, one gradually discovers, not just to see what it is like, or because they have seen and have chosen to return, but because circumstances in their wonderful, lucid way have combined to send them there.

My roommates—I can't afford a whole stateroom—have usually detested their destinations from experience or dreaded them from hearsay. One, a silent, earnest-looking young man who was fond of playing solitaire and reading the poems of Edgar Allan Poe, always spent his winters in the hot countries, not because he liked them, but because his profession of " looping the loop " on a bicycle could be continuously pursued only in climates salubrious to the circus. Another, a grizzled old Wisconsin timber cruiser, was being sent, much against his will, to make a report on some Cuban forest lands.

" It is a queer, strange thing," he confided in me when we parted in Havana harbor, " that a man of my age and morals won't be able even to get drunk without the help o' that "—and he nodded toward the ladylike little interpreter who had come out to meet him and take charge of him during his stay.

Still another struck me at first as a provincial and tedious New Englander until I found out his mission. His inside coat pocket was stuffed with photographs of his numerous children, and he had a horror of snakes and tarantulas that he often expressed much as one of Miss Wilkins's heroines might express her horror of mice. Like all persons who share the same dread and are about to make a first visit to the tropics, he conferred on reptiles and poisonous insects a kind of civic importance that they themselves under no circumstances assume. He had a haunting idea that the entire toxical population of Guatemala would be lined up at the railway station to receive him. But when it came out that he was being sent twenty-six hundred miles for the sole purpose of splicing a rope—a matter, he said, of a few hours at the most—I was compelled to see him in a light not only different but almost romantic. Somewhere in darkest Guatemala there was a rope four and a half miles long. It broke, and my roommate, who had never been farther south than Summer Street nor farther west than West Newton—localities between which he had vibrated daily for many years—was, it seemed, the one human being among all the human beings from Guatemala to Boston who was capable of splicing it. As the rope had cost three thousand dollars it was distinctly less expensive to import a West Newtonian than to import another rope.

Then, too, I once between Havana and Vera Cruz had as a roommate a "confidence man"—a broadening and therefore a valuable experience. One is not often given the privilege of living for five days with a confidence man on terms of confidence. He was a tall, lank, sandy-haired creature of about forty, with a Roman nose, a splendid mustache, unemotional, gray-green eyes, a diamond ring, and suspenders, as well as a belt; the sort of looking person whom twenty-five years ago British playwrights would have seized upon as "a typical American." In a bloodless fashion his whole existence was "a carnival of crime"—a succession of scurvy tricks, heartless swindles, lies, frauds, and, now and then, candid, undisguised thefts. Sometimes, as when he sold jewelry and bric-a-brac at auction, his dealings were with the semi-intelligent well-to-do, but more often he exerted himself among the credulous poor, as when he unloaded brass watch cases filled with tacks on negroes at Texas fairs. His marked playing cards and loaded dice, which he showed and explained to me with much amiable vanity, were very ingenious, and I found our long, cheerful discussions on the technic of his art most helpful. His contributions to them, in fact, threw upon certain phases of sociology a brilliant and authoritative light that I defy anyone to get out of a book or put into it. From instinct, from habit, from love of the work, he was an almost thoroughly consistent scoundrel, and it was a shock to discover by the end of the voyage that the thing about him I most objected to was his wearing suspenders as well as a belt.

There is always a brave and hopeful little band of actors on board — usually an American stock company on the way to its financial and artistic doom in the City of Mexico. And it is invariably named after the beautiful young lady who has hypnotized some middle-aged Mexican patron saint of the drama into guaranteeing everybody six weeks' salary and a return ticket. If it isn't the Beryl Smith Company it is sure to be the Company of Hazel Jones or Gladys Robinson, and Beryl (or Hazel or Gladys) is so beautiful that she can stand unhatted and unveiled in the midday sunlight of the Gulf—beauty knows no more merciless test— without making you wish she wouldn't. Furthermore, you continue to think her hair the loveliest color you have ever seen, even after—with an extremely elegant gesture—she tosses her chewing

7

gum overboard and languidly tells you how she does it.

But her tragedy, like that of her more hard-working associates, is a great inability to hold any-one's attention except when she is off the stage. If actors could only arrange in some way to charge admission to their semi-private existence, acting as a profession would be less of a gamble. For it is an unexplained fact that, however obscure, incon-spicuous, and well-behaved they may be, actors and actresses excite, when they are not acting, more curiosity, speculation, and comment than any other class. Start the rumor on shipboard that a certain quiet, unattached young woman, who wears a shabby mackintosh, common-sense shoes and a last year's hat, is a third-rate actress, and the center of the deck at once becomes hers. A few days later, how-ever, when she turns out to be a first-rate physician or the professor of Pre-Christian Hebrew literature at Bryn Mawr, her value as a conversational re-source drops instantly to nothing.

But if on the voyage to Mexico one's compatriots strike, to fall back on the cant phrase, a diverting " note," the Cubans, the Spaniards, the Yucatecans, and the Mexicans in general strike whole chords. To set sail for anywhere, even Duluth, has always seemed to me considerably more than merely a practical step toward transporting myself from one place to another. On going aboard a ship I can't—and would not if I could—rid myself of the sensation that there is something improbable and adventurous about me; that everybody, from the captain to the sixty-year-old cockney stewardess, is about to engage in "deeds of love and high emprise." The sudden translation from Forty-second Street to the deck of any steamer bound for foreign parts has a thrill in it, but if the destination be the tropics, there is more than one. They are incited by the presence of so many slim, sallow, gesticulating men, and stout, powdered, gayly (and badly) dressed women, by the surprisingly variegated inflections and minor cadences of the Spanish language, by the first penetrating whiff of exotic tobacco smoke from the cigarette of a coffee-colored old lady with a mustache, from the very shape and quality of the luggage as it is hoisted over the side or carried up by the army of negro porters; the most un-Anglo-Saxon luggage conceivable. They travel, the Latin-Americans, with incredible amounts of it, and the sight of it always makes me wonder whether they have ever traveled before or ever expect to travel again. For it consists chiefly of gigantic, smashed-in paper band-boxes, satchels precariously fashioned out of something that tries hard to look like leather and doesn't in the least succeed, pale blue or pink trunks that for some occult reason are narrower at the bottom than at the top and might be either small, frivolous coffins or large, forbidding cradles, corpulent bales of heaven knows what covered with matting, baskets covered with newspapers, articles of wearing apparel covered with confusion, and fifty other things covered with nothing at all. Once at the Wall Street wharf I saw a young Mexican get out of a Holland House omnibus bearing in his hand a parrot cage stuffed full of shoes. It seemed to me at the time a delirious incident, and I remembered it. But I doubt that, after having lived in Mexico, I should now notice or remember it at all. He was a very charming young person whose mother had been a lady in waiting to the Empress Carlotta, and he was on his way back from Belgium, where he goes once a year to sink on his knee and kiss the aged Carlotta's hand.

Oh, yes, there is always a thrill in it—this setting sail for the hot countries. It begins on the dock, slightly increases as one steams past the low, monotonous coast of Florida, becomes disturbing in the exquisite little harbor of Havana, and at Progreso, where for thirty-six hours one stares at the shallow, green gulf water, the indolent sharks and the stretch of sand and palm trees wavering in heat, that is Yucatan, it enslaves one like a drug of which one disapproves, but to which one nevertheless succumbs. One afternoon at sunset, before we had even sighted land, a little French boy accurately summed up for us the vague and various sensations that, during the last few hours of the hot afternoon, had stolen over us all. He had been born in Yucatan and was returning there with his father after a first visit to France. Suddenly in his race around the deck with some other children he stopped short, glanced at the group of half-dozing, half-fanning women in steamer chairs, at the listless men against the rail, at the calm, lemon-colored sky and the floating islands of seaweed on the green water. Then, throwing back his head, he closed his eyes, drew a long appreciative breath and, with his eyes still closed, exclaimed luxuriously: "Ah-h-h, on sent les pays chauds!"

II

AT first you are both amazed and annoyed by what seems like not only lack of curiosity but positive ignorance on the part of Americans who live in Mexico. As a new arrival, I had an admirable thirst for information which I endeavored to slake at what I supposed were fountains of knowledge as well as of afternoon tea. The tea was delicious and plentiful; but the knowledge simply did not exist.

"What is the population of Barranca?" you ask of an intelligent compatriot who has lived in Barranca for ten years.

"Why, I don't know exactly," he replies, as if the question were an interesting one that had never before occurred to him.

"Oh, I don't mean exactly—but is it eight thousand, or fourteen, or twenty-five? It's rather difficult for a stranger to form an idea; the towns are built so differently from ours. Although they may not be really large, they are so compact that they look more populous and 'citified' than places of the same size in the United States," you explain.

"Yes, that's very true, and it *is* difficult," he agrees.

"Do you suppose I could find out anywhere? Do they ever take the census?" you pursue.

"The census? Why, I don't know about that. But there's Smith on the bench over there having his shoes shined. He's been in the country for fifteen years—he'll be able to tell you. Smith, I want to introduce a friend of mine who is very anxious to know the population of Barranca and whether they ever take the census."

"The census?" muses Smith, ignoring the population entirely. "I don't know if they take the census, but they take your taxes with great regularity," he declares with a laugh. Then follows a pleasant ten minutes with Smith, during which the reason of your introduction to him does not recur, and after precisely the same thing has happened several other times with several other persons, you would almost rather start a revolution than an inquiry into the population of Barranca.

The specific instance is perhaps a trivial one, but it is typical, and, as I said, you are for a time amazed and irritated, on asking intelligent questions about the federal and state governments, the judiciary, the army, education, morality, and even so obvious a matter as the climate, to receive from American acquaintances replies that are never accurate and rarely as much as inaccurately definite. Some of them frankly admit that, as they never have had personal relations with the establishments you seek to learn about (barring the climate), they have not taken the trouble to inform themselves. Others appear to experience a belated regret at their long indifference, promise to look the matter up and let you know. But they never do, and it is rather discouraging. You yearn to acquire a respectably comprehensive idea of the conditions in which you are living, yet the only people with whom you can carry on any but a most staccato and indispensable conversation are unable to throw light. So, being the only one really intelligent foreigner in the republic, you resort to the medium of art, and begin to read books.

Everyone you know has at some time or other read and enjoyed Prescott's " Conquest," but it does not emerge that on the subject of Mexico they have ever read anything else, and for a while you quietly revel in your mental alertness and superior intelligence. You are learning all about the country

14

—its institutions and laws, its products and habits —while your listless friends still sit in darkness. Then one fine morning something happens—something of no especial importance, but something that nevertheless serves to insert the thin edge of suspicion's wedge between you and your learning.

You have, for instance, read that "in virtue of the constitution adopted February 5, 1857, arrest is prohibited, save in the case of crimes meriting corporal punishment," and it has seemed to you a wise and just provision. You have also, let us say, employed two competent stone masons to build a coffee tank, a fireplace, a pigpen, or some such useful accessory of life in the tropics, and you become much disturbed when, after they have worked steadily and well for three or four days, they fail to appear. That afternoon as you stroll through the plaza lamenting their perfidy, you are astonished at receiving two friendly, sheepish greetings from two sheepish, friendly stone masons who are engaged in laying municipal cobblestones, together with thirty or forty other prisoners, under the eyes of several heavily armed policemen. Unmistakably they are your masons, and with much bewilderment you demand of Smith—who, no doubt, is strolling with you—just what it means.

15

"It merely means," Smith explains, "that the town is repairing part of the plaza pavement and needs competent masons. So they arrested yours."

"But on what grounds?"

"Oh, drunkenness probably."

"Do you suppose they were drunk? They seemed like very steady men."

"Why, they may have been a trifle elated," Smith laughs. "The assumption that they were isn't a particularly startling one in this part of the world. But that wasn't why they were arrested. They were arrested because they were good masons and the city happens to need them. If they hadn't been drunk, some one would have been sent out to make them so—never, unfortunately, a very arduous undertaking."

"Oh, indeed; how simple and efficacious!" you murmur, and go home to read some more.

Still other wise and just provisions of the same excellent document are that no person may be obliged to work for another person without freely consenting so to work, nor without receiving just remuneration, and that imprisonment for debts of a purely civil nature is prohibited. But as your Spanish gradually improves and you are able to have more sustained talks with the natives, you learn that the entire lives of a great number of peones working on haciendas contain two alternatives, one of which is practical slavery and the other imprisonment for debt to his employer.

A young man goes to work on, say, a sugar plantation for the magnificent wages of thirty-six Mexican cents a day. In the course of time—usually a very short time—he acquires a family. If he acquires it after certain preliminary formalities, such as a marriage ceremony and its attendant festivities, his employer has loaned him the forty or fifty pesos—unpayable sum—necessary to defray the costs of the priest and the piper, and the young man's eternal indebtedness begins from the beginning. If, however, there are no formalities, the financial burden is not assumed until the birth of the first child.

Mexicans of every station adore their children, and even when, as frequently happens among the lower classes, the parents are neither civilly nor religiously married (in Mexico only the civil ceremony is recognized by the law) nothing is too good or too expensive for the offspring. They are baptized and, if the informal union of the parents lasts long enough, they are confirmed. But in Mexico, as elsewhere, the kingdom of heaven costs money,

17

and this money the young man's employer cheerfully advances. Then in the natural march of events some one dies. Death, of course, all the world over, has become one of our grossest extravagances. Again the employer delightedly pays.

Now he has the young man—no longer so young —exactly where 'his sugar plantation wants him. On thirty-six cents a day there is no possibility of a laborer's paying a debt of a hundred or more pesos and moving away, and if he attempts to depart without paying it, a word from the hacendado to his friend the jefe político would suffice to land him in jail and keep him there. It is impossible to deny that on some haciendas, perhaps on many, this form of slavery is a happier, a more comfortable arrangement than would be the freedom so energetically insisted on in the constitution. Still, slavery is neither a pretty word nor a pretty idea, and yet, in spite of the constitution, the idea obtains in Mexico quite as it obtains in the United States.

Then again you read with satisfaction that among other forms of freedom—" freedom of education, freedom to exercise the liberal professions, freedom of thought," and so on—the freedom of the press is guaranteed; guaranteed, that is to say, with the reservation that " private rights and the public peace shall not be violated." The manner in which this reservation can be construed, however, does not occur to you until you read in *El Imparcial* or in the *Mexican Herald*—the best Spanish and American daily papers—an account of, let us say, a strike of the mill operatives at Orizaba, and then, a week later, chance to learn what actually happened.

"I see by the *Herald* that you had a little strike at Orizaba the other day," you remark to the middle-aged British manager of a large Orizaba jute mill, with whom you find yourself in the same swimming pond at the baths of Tehuacan. "The *Herald* said that in a clash with the troops several strikers were killed and twenty-five were injured."

"Did it indeed?" remarks the manager dryly, and later, when you are sitting together in the sun after your bath, he explains that the strike was an incipient revolution engineered by a junta in St. Louis, that the Government sent down a regiment from the City of Mexico, that in an impromptu sort of way six hundred strikers were immediately shot, and that the next morning thirty-four were formally, elaborately, and officially executed. This prompt and heroic measure, he informs you, ended both the strike and the incipient revolution, and as you compare what you have read in the papers with what is the truth, you can tell yourself that it has also ended your illusions as to the freedom of the Mexican press.

In fact you begin to realize why, when you ask American residents of the country for information, their replies are usually so vague, so contradictory, so uninforming. It is not, as a rule, because they know too little, but because they know too much. Theoretical Mexico—the Mexico of constitutions, reform laws, statutes, and books of travel—has ceased, long since, vitally to concern them. It is Mexico as they day by day find it that interests them and that in the least counts. And practical, every-day Mexico is an entirely different, infinitely more mysterious, fascinating affair.

" Does it rain here in summer as much as it does in winter?" I once asked a Mexican lady in a saturated mountain village in the State of Vera Cruz.

" No hay reglas fijas, señor " (there are no fixed rules), she replied, after a thoughtful silence, with a shrug.

No hay reglas fijas! It is not perhaps a detailed description of the great Don Porfirio's republic, but it is a consummate epitome, and once you have committed it to memory and "taken it to heart," your literary pursuits begin to languish. After traveling for three weeks in Mexico, almost anyone can write an entertaining and oracular volume, but after living there for several years, the oracle—unless subsidized by the Government—has a tendency to become dumb. For, in a country where theory and practice are so at variance, personal experience becomes the chart by which one is accustomed to steer, and although it is a valuable one, it may, for a hundred quaint reasons, be entirely different from that of the man whose ranch, or mine, or coffee place adjoins one's own.

In just this, I feel sure, lies much of the indisputable charm of Mexico. No hay reglas fijas. Everyone's experience is different, and everyone, in a sense, is a pioneer groping his way—like Cortés on his prodigious march up from the sea. One never knows, from the largest to the smallest circumstances of life, just what to expect, and Ultimate Truth abideth not. This is not so much because Mexicans are instinctive and facile liars, as because the usual methods of ascertaining and disseminating news are not employed. At home we demand facts and get them. In Mexico one subsists on rumor and never demands anything. A well-regulated, systematic, and precise person always detests Mexico and can rarely bring himself to say a kind word about anything in it, including the scenery. But if one is not inclined to exaggerate the importance of exactitude and is perpetually interested in the casual, the florid, and the problematic, Mexico is one long, carelessly written but absorbing romance.

III

SUPERFICIALLY, Mexico is a prolonged romance. For even its brutal realities—of which there are many—are the realities of an intensely pictorial people among surroundings that, to Northern eyes, are never quite commonplace. I once, for instance, saw a plucky little policeman shoot and kill an insanely drunken shoemaker who, in the marketplace a few minutes before, apropos of nothing except the fact that he *was* insanely drunk, had cut the throat of a young milkman. The policeman pursued him in his mad flight for home and, just as they passed me on a deserted street near the outskirts of the town, returned a quick stab in the stomach from the shoemaker's knife (still reeking with the milkman's blood) by a revolver shot. They then both collapsed in a mud puddle, and to me was appointed the rôle of arousing the neighborhood, unbuttoning the policeman's clothes and slipping two pillows under his pale, brave head.

Of course it was the most squalid of incidents;

precisely what happens every little while in New York and Pittsburg and San Francisco, and every few minutes, so we are told, in Chicago. But in Barranca, somehow, the squalor of the affair could not successfully compete with the dramatic interest and the stage-setting. The people who emerged from their blue and pink and yellow and green houses at my alarm (no one in Mexico is alarmed by the sound of firearms) the distracted widow— who, however, postponed complete distraction until after she had carefully gone through her dead husband's pockets—the pompous arrival of the chief of police, the color and costuming and arrangement of it all, were far too like the last scenes of " Carmen " or " Cavalleria Rusticana " to permit of one's experiencing any but an agreeably theatrical sensation of horror.

I strolled away after the shoemaker was removed to the police station and the canvas-covered litter had been sent back for the gasping policeman, asking myself by what strange alchemy drunkenness, murder, and retribution in a mud puddle could be made so entertaining. The brutish spectacle, I realized, ought to have shocked me, and the remainder of my walk should have been spent in reflecting that the world was a very wicked place.

But I had not been shocked at all, and the world just then seemed not so much wicked as unusually interesting. And this, I flatter myself, was not on my part a moral obtuseness, but an innate quality of the general Mexican scene. For it is always pictorial and always dramatic; it is not only invariably a painting, but the kind of painting that tells a story. Paintings that tell stories are declared by critics to be " bad art." Perhaps this is why so many travelers in Mexico find so little to admire.

At first, I confess, almost everybody in the republic looks like a home-made cigar. But when your eyes have become properly focused, it is difficult to remember having thought of so cheap a comparison. Whether your relations with the people be agreeable or otherwise, you cannot but admit, after becoming used to the type, that there is among all classes an extraordinary amount of beauty. In every Mexican crowd there are, naturally, a great many ugly persons and plain persons and average-looking persons. An omnipotent Creator for, no doubt, some perfectly good reason that surpasseth all my little understanding, chooses, in perpetuating the human race, to depart, as a rule, very far from perfection and even from charm. But in Mexico, although the departure can be as far, it is somehow not as frequent.

In its way, the mixture of Spaniard and tropical Indian—which was the original recipe for making the contemporary Mexican—is physically a pleasing one. It isn't our way, but one doesn't after a while find it less attractive for that. The Indians, in the part of Mexico I happen to know best, have at least the outward characteristics of a " gentle " race. Even when they are tall, they are inevitably and—one might almost say—incorrigibly plump. One never ceases to marvel at the superhuman strength existing beneath the pretty and effeminate modeling of their arms and legs and backs. Except when they grow old and wither up, which they do, like all tropical races, while they are still young, they yet display no angles. However great may be their muscular development from trotting up and down perpendicular mountain trails with incredible loads of corn, or pottery, or tiles, or firewood, or human beings on their backs, the muscles themselves never stand out. The legs of an American " strong man " look usually like an anatomical chart, but the legs of the most powerful Totonac Indian—and the power of many of them is beyond belief—would serve admirably as one of those idealized extremities on which women's hosiery is displayed in shop windows. In spite of their constantly surprising exhibitions both of unpremeditated strength and long endurance, there is in the general aspect of their physique more of prettiness than of vigor, more grace than virility.

With these people and others like them, the Spaniards began to mingle in the year 1519, and from the union of Spanish men and aboriginal women sprang the Mexican of to-day. In them the physical traits of both races are obvious. If, by alliance, the native lost some of his round, sleek modeling, the conqueror renounced much of his gauntness and austerity. For the modern Mexican, roughly speaking, is neither a rugged type nor an unmanly one. He is, as a rule, a " spare," small-waisted creature whose muscles, when he has any, show—unlike those of the pure Indian—in the ordinary way, but whose small feet and slender, beautiful hands are deceptive. A cargador of my acquaintance, whose hands are like those of a slim girl, and who, if he wore shoes, would require a narrow five, thinks nothing of transporting on his back from the railway station to the center of the town, a distance of more than a mile up a steep hill, a gigantic trunk (the kind that used to be known as a "Saratoga"), a smaller trunk, half a dozen "dress-suit cases," a bundle of rugs, and a steamer chair. They by no means lack strength, but it is more often than not concealed in a body all sallow slenderness and grace. And gracefulness in a nation is a characteristic no good American fresh from "God's country"—whatever that patriotic if strangely un-Christian phrase may mean— can in his heart of hearts forgive. The typical Mexican, although not effeminately, is delicately formed, and, in addition to the prevailing lightness and sensitiveness of his structure, a great factor in the general high average of his good looks is the almost complete elimination of the matter of complexion.

With Northern races it is difficult to disassociate the thought of beauty in either sex from a certain clear glowing quality of the epidermis known as " a complexion." But in Mexico this consideration— in spite of the quarter of an inch of powder which the ladies of the upper classes apply to their faces on a substratum of glycerin—does not enter. You know that even under the powder all Mexican complexions approximate a satisfactory café au lait standard, and that, if the owners are not positively suffering from smallpox, they are all good. They impress you, after your eyes become acclimated, as being an extraordinarily ornamental race, and it is always amusing to notice that, however strong may be the aversion to them of an American or British resident, he cannot refrain now and then from an involuntary tribute to their unconscious habit of quietly or violently " composing " themselves at every moment of their lives into some kind of a frameable picture.

" I hate 'em all," an American building contractor once exclaimed to me with deep sincerity. " But," he added, " after my work is over for the day, I like to sit on a bench in the plaza and look at 'em. I sit there a couple of hours every evening. Even when the rascals ain't doing anything in particular, you always sort of feel as if there was something doing."

This feeling—for the accurate description of which I was truly grateful—is largely responsible in Mexico for the plaza and balcony habit that one immediately acquires and that becomes one's chief form of diversion. In a small city of the United States or in England, even a person of unlimited leisure would have to be doddering, or an invalid or a tramp, before he would consent to sit daily for two or three hours on a bench in a public square, or lean over a balcony watching the same people pursue their ordinary vocations in the street below. The monotony of the thing, the procession's dead level of prosperous mediocrity, would very soon prove intolerable, and he would find some one, anyone, to talk to or endeavor to forget himself in a book or a newspaper.

In Mexico, however, complete idleness is rarely a bore. "Even when the rascals ain't doing anything in particular, you always sort of feel as if there was something doing." One afternoon in a small Mexican town I kept tab from my balcony on what, for about eight minutes, took place in the street below. Although the town was small and the day an unusually quiet one, owing to a fiesta in the neighborhood to which many of the inhabitants had gone, there was no dearth of incident against the usual background of big-hatted cargadores waiting for employment in the middle of the street; of burros, each with four large cobblestones in a box on its back; of biblical-looking girls (an endless stream of them) bearing huge waterjars to and from a circular fountain lined with pale-blue tiles; of old men who wail at intervals that they are selling pineapple ice cream; of old women with handfuls of white and yellow and

green lottery tickets; of basket sellers and sellers of
flowers (the kind of adorable bouquets that haven't
been seen anywhere else since the early seventies;
composed of damp moss, tinfoil, toothpicks, a lace
petticoat, a wooden handle, and, yes, some flowers
arranged in circles according to color); of mozos
who you feel sure have been sent on an errand and
told to "come right back," but who have apparently no intention of returning for several hours;
of ladies draped in black lace on their way to meditate in church; of hundreds of other leisurely moving figures that were as a bright-colored, shifting
chorus to the more striking episodes.

Item one (so runs my page of hasty notes):
Three rather fragile-looking young men swinging
along with a grand piano on their heads. Under
my window they all stop a moment to let one of
them ask a passerby to stick a cigarette in his mouth
and light it, which is duly done.

Item two: A flock of sheep followed by a
shepherd in clean white cotton with a crimson
sarape around his shoulders. He looks like Ved-
der's Lazarus. The sheep have just piled into the
open door of the hotel and are trying to come upstairs. In the excitement a new-born lamb has its
leg hurt. The shepherd gathers it in his arms,

wraps it in the sarape, thoughtfully kisses it twice on the head and proceeds.

Item three: A funeral. As there are only three streets in this place that aren't built up and down a mountain side, there are no vehicles, and coffins, like everything else, are carried on men's backs. This is an unusually expensive coffin, but then of course the silver handles are only hired for the occasion. They'll be removed at the grave, as otherwise they would be dug up and stolen. I wonder why women so rarely go to funerals here? There is a string of men a block long, but no women. Some of them (probably relatives) have in their hands lighted candles tied with crape. They are nice, fat candles and don't blow out. Everybody in the street takes his hat off as the cortége passes.

Item four: The daily pack train of mules from the Concepción sugar hacienda. There must be two hundred and fifty of them, and their hoofs clatter on the cobblestones like magnified hail. The street is jammed with them, and where the sidewalk narrows to almost nothing, people are trying to efface themselves against the wall. A wonderful exhibition of movement and color in the blazing sunlight: the warm seal-brown of the mules, the paler yellow-brown of the burlap in which are wrapped the conical sugar loaves (eight to a mule), with the arrieros in yellow straw hats, brilliant blue shirts and scarlet waist bandas bringing up the rear.

Item five: A dog fight.

Item six: Another and much worse dog fight.

Item seven: An Indian woman with apparently a whole poultry farm half concealed upon her person. She calls up to ask if I would like to buy a chicken. Why on earth should a young man on a balcony of a hotel bedroom like to buy a chicken?

Item eight: An acquaintance makes a megaphone of his hands and inquires if I am very busy. I reply, " Yes, frightfully," and we adjourn to the plaza for the afternoon.

IV

THE inability of people in general to think for themselves—the inevitableness with which they welcome an opinion, a phrase, a catchword, if it be sufficiently indiscriminating and easy to remember, and the fashion in which they then solemnly echo it, are never more displayed than when they are commenting upon a race not their own. Sometimes this rubber-stamp sort of criticism is eulogistic in tone as when, for instance, a few years ago it was impossible in the United States to speak of the Japanese without calling forth from some tedious sounding-board, who couldn't have told a Jap from a Filipino, the profound exclamation: "What a wonderful little people they are!" But more often than not, ignorant criticism of a foreign country is also adverse. For one nation cannot altogether understand another, and if it is true that "to understand everything is to pardon everything," it must also be true that unforgiveness is one of the penalties of being misunderstood.

It is the vast throng of fairly well educated

34

"people in general" who are forever divulging the news that "Englishmen have no sense of humor," that "the French are very immoral," that "all Italians steal and none of them wash," that "every German eats with his knife and keeps his bedroom windows closed at night," that "the inhabitants of Russia are barbarians with a veneer of civilization" (how they cherish that word "veneer"!), and that "the Scotch are stingy."

The formula employed in the case of Mexicans runs usually something like this: "They're the laziest people in the world, and although they seem to treat you politely they are all treacherous and dishonest. Their politeness is merely on the surface; it doesn't come from the heart"—as does the exquisite courtesy we are so accustomed to receive from everybody in the United States, one is tempted to add, without, however, doing so. For what, after all, is the use of entering into a discussion with the sort of person who supposes that his own or anyone's else politeness "comes from the heart," or has, in fact, anything to do with the heart? Politeness, of course, is, all the world over, just the pleasing surface quality we should expect it to be from the derivation of the word. Even in Kansas or South Boston we do not necessarily wish to die for the old gentleman whom we allow to pass through the doorway first, and the act of taking off one's hat to a lady scarcely convicts one of a secret passion for her. But it is odd what depths are demanded of Mexican politeness, which—except for the fact that there is much more of it—is, like our own, an outward "polish" and nothing else.

If, however, there is anything valuable in politeness as such, the Mexicans have over us at least one extensive advantage. For in Mexico the habit of politeness in its most elaborate form is so universal that the very occasional lack of it in anybody gives one the sensation of being not only surprised but somewhat hurt. If, for instance, a street-car conductor in taking my ticket should fail to say "Thank you," and neglect on receiving it to make toward me a short, quick gesture of the hand—something between a wave and flourish—I should realize that, as far as I was concerned, his manners had not risen to the ordinary standard, and wonder why he had chosen to be indifferent and rather rude. This naturally would not apply in the City of Mexico, where, as in all great capitals, the mixture of nationalities has had a noticeable influence upon many native characteristics.

But in provincial Mexico—wherever there was a street car—it would be true.

In riding along a country road it is likely to be considered an example of gringo brutalidad if one does not speak to every man, woman, and child one meets or overtakes. And completely to fulfill the requirements of rural etiquette, the greeting must be not collective but individual; everybody in one group murmurs something—usually " Adiós "—for the especial benefit of everybody in the other. The first time I took part in this—as it seemed to me then—extraordinary performance, my party of three had met another party of equal number on a narrow path in the mountains, and as we scraped past one another, the word adiós in tired but distinct tones was uttered exactly eighteen times—a positive litany of salutation that nearly caused me to roll off my mule. It is a polite sociable custom and I like it, but under certain circumstances it can become more exhausting than one would suppose. In approaching—on Sunday afternoon, toward the end of a long hot ride—a certain little town (which no doubt is to-day very much as it was when Cortés three hundred and eighty-seven years ago mentioned it in one of his letters to Charles V) I have met as many as three hundred persons returning from market to their ranchitos and villages. Adiós is a beautiful word, but—well, after one has said it and nothing else with a parched throat and an air of sincerity for the three hundredth time, one no longer much cares. However, if you don't know the returning marketers it is safe to assume that they all know a great deal about you, and for a variety of reasons it is well, however tired one may be, to observe the convention.

With the pure-blooded Indians along the Gulf coast there is, when they happen to know you, an elaborateness about your meetings and partings on the road that amounts to a kind of ritual. The sparkling conversation that follows is an ordinary example and an accurate translation of what is said. During its progress, hands are grasped and shaken several times—the number being in direct ratio to the number of drinks your friend has had during the day.

"Good day, Don Carlitos. How are you?"

"Good day, Vicente" (or Guadalupe or Ipifigenio). "Very well, thank you. How are you?"

"Thanks to God, there is no change! How are Don Guillermo and your mamma?"

"Many thanks, they are as always." (A pause.) "The roads are bad."

" Yes, señor, very bad. Is there much coffee? "

" Enough."

" I am coming to pick next week." (He really isn't and he knows I know he isn't—but the remark delicately suggests that there is no ill feeling.)

" Come when you wish to. Well, until we meet again."

" Until we meet again—if God wishes it. May you go with God! "

" Many thanks, Vicente " (or Ipifigenio or Guadalupe). " Remain with God! "

" Thank you, señor—if God wishes it."

" Adiós."

" Adiós."

Toward women we are everywhere accustomed to a display of more or less politeness, but in Mexico, under the ordinary circumstances of life, men of all classes are polite to one another. Acquaintances take off their hats both when they meet and part, and I have heard a half-naked laborer bent double under a sack of coffee-berries murmur, " With your permission," as he passed in front of a bricklayer who was repairing a wall. Even the children—who are not renowned in other lands for observing any particular code of etiquette among themselves—treat one another, as a rule, with an

astonishing consideration. Once in the plaza at
Tehuacan I found myself behind three little boys
of about six or seven who were sedately strolling
around and around while the band played, quite
in the manner of their elders. One of them had
a cent, and after asking the other two how they
would most enjoy having it invested, he bought
from a dulcero one of those small, fragile creations
of egg and sugar known, I believe, as a "kiss."
This he at once undertook to divide, with the result that when the guests had each received a pinch
of the ethereal structure, there was nothing left for
the host but two or three of his own sticky little
fingers. He looked a trifle surprised for a moment, and I thought it would be only natural and
right for him to demand a taste of the others. But
instead of that he merely licked his fingers in
silence and then resumed the promenade where it
had been left off. However, the general seraphic-
ness of Mexican children is a chapter in itself.

"Is that your horse?" you ask of a stranger
with whom you have entered into conversation on
the road.

"No, señor—it is yours," he is likely to reply
with a slight bow. And perhaps it is by reason of
formulæ like this that the great public characterizes

Mexican politeness as "all on the surface—not from the heart." The stranger's answer, naturally, is just a pretty phrase. But all politeness is largely verbal and the only difference between the politeness of Mexico and the politeness of other countries consists of the fact that, first, the Spanish language is immensely rich in pretty phrases, and, secondly, that literally everyone makes use of them.

One of the most amusing manifestations of the state of mind known as "patriotism" is the fact that every nation is thoroughly convinced of the dishonesty of every other. From end to end of Europe the United States is, and for a long time has been, a synonym of political and financial corruption. We are popularly supposed to be a nation of sharks who have all grown fabulously rich by the simple, effective method of eating one another—and everybody else—up. This is not perhaps the topic the French ambassador picks out to expound at White House dinners, nor does it form the burden of the Duke of Abruzzi's remarks on the occasion of planting a tree at Washington's tomb. It is merely a conviction of the great majority of their fellow countrymen at home. On the other hand, very few persons with a drop of Anglo-Saxon blood in them can bring themselves to admit—

much less to feel—that the "Latin" races have
any but a shallow and versatile conception of honesty and truth. It is a provision of nature that
one's own people should have a monopoly of all
the virtues. Uncle John, who was given short
change for a napoleon by a waiter at the Jardin
de Paris, is more than sustained in his original
opinion of the French. And Aunt Lizzie, who paid
a dollar and a half for a trunk strap at the leading harness shop of Pekin, Illinois, and then had it
stolen at the Laredo customhouse, will all her life
believe that the chief occupation of everyone in
Mexico, from President Diaz down, is the theft
of trunk straps. This sounds like trifling—but it
is the way in which one country's opinion of another is really formed.

A discussion of the comparative honesty of na-
tions must always be a futile undertaking, as a
considerable number of persons in every country
are dishonest. I know for a fact that when Aunt
Lizzie alighted at Laredo to have her trunk ex-
amined, she saw the strap "with her own eyes,"
and that somewhere between the border and her
final destination it miraculously disappeared. On
the other hand, I always leave everything I own
scattered about my room in Mexican hotels, be-

cause I am lazy, and various articles that I should regret to lose I have sometimes forgotten to pack, because I am careless. But nothing has ever been stolen from me in Mexico, and when I have requested the innkeeper by letter or telegram, " Please to send me the two diamond tiaras together with the emerald stomacher I inadvertently left in the second drawer of the washstand," they have invariably come to me by return express—neither of which experiences (Aunt Lizzie's and mine) proves anything whatever about anybody.

The question of "laziness" would be easy to dispose of if one could simply say that just as there are honest and dishonest Mexicans, there are indolent and energetic Mexicans. But somehow one can't. Many of them are extremely industrious, many of them work, when they do work, as hard and as long as it is possible for human beings to bear fatigue—and yet, of what we know as "energy," I have seen little or nothing. For whatever may be the word's precise definition, it expresses to most of us an adequate power operating under the lash of a perpetual desire to get something done. In Mexico there are many kinds of adequate power, but apparently the desire to get anything done does not exist. The inhabitants, from peon to professional man, conduct their affairs as if everybody were going "to live," as Marcus Aurelius says, "ten thousand years!"

Among the lower classes, even leaving out of consideration the influence of a tropical and semitropical climate, it is not difficult to account for this lack of energy. No people whose diet consists chiefly of tortillas, chile, black coffee, and cigarettes are ever going to be lashed by the desire to accomplish. This is the diet of babies as soon as they are weaned. I have heard proud mothers at country dances compare notes, while their men were playing monte around a kerosene torch stuck in the ground.

"My little boy"—aged three—"won't *look* at a tortilla unless it is covered with chile," one of them explains.

"Does he cry for coffee?" inquires another. "My baby"—aged two and a half—"screams and cries unless we give her coffee three and four times a day." It is not surprising that a population perpetually in the throes of intestinal disorder should be somewhat lacking in energy.

Furthermore, they are a religious, or rather a superstitious people, given to observing as many of the innumerable feasts on the calendar as is compatible with making both ends approach—one hesitates to say meet. The entire working force of an isolated ranch will abruptly cease from its labors on hearing from some meddlesome passerby that in more populous localities the day is being celebrated. That it is, may or may not be a fact, and if a supply of liquor cannot be procured there is no very definite way of enjoying unpremeditated idleness. But a fiesta is a fiesta, and everyone stands about all day unwilling to work, unable to play—the prey of ennui and capricious tempers.

Possibly it is mere hair splitting to draw a distinction between laziness and lack of energy, but although climate and heredity will abide and continue to restrain the lower classes from undue continuity of effort, even as they still do the wealthy and educated, it is not fantastic to believe that education and a more nourishing, less emotional diet (both are on the way) will stimulate in the Mexican people some of the latent qualities that will absolve them from the popular reproach of laziness.

V

ONE December morning, while I was aimlessly strolling in the white, dry sunlight of Puebla, I wandered into the cathedral. The semireligious, semiculinary festival known as Christmas had come and gone for me in Jalapa, but as soon as I went into the church and walked beyond the choir, the awkward situation of which in Spanish cathedrals shows on the part of catholics an unusual indifference to general impressiveness, it was apparent—gorgeously, overwhelmingly apparent—that here Christmas still lingered. This cathedral is always gorgeous and always somewhat overpowering, for, unlike any other I can recall, that which, perhaps, was the original scheme of decoration looks as if it had been completed a few moments before one's arrival. We have learned to expect in these places worn surfaces, tarnished gilt, a sense of invisible dust and tones instead of colors. So few of them look as they were intended to look that, just as we prefer Greek statues unpainted, we prefer the decorations of cathedrals to be in the

46

nature of exquisite effacement. In the great church of Puebla, however, little is exquisite and certainly nothing is effaced. On entering, one is at first only surprised that an edifice so respectably old can be so jauntily new. But when, during mass, one passes slightly before the choir, and is confronted by the first possible view of any amplitude, it is something more than rhetoric to say that for a moment the cathedral of Puebla is overpowering.

The use of gold leaf in decoration is like money. A little is pleasant, merely too much is vulgar; but a positively staggering amount of it seems to justify itself. My own income is not vulgar; neither is Mr. Rockefeller's. The ordinary white and gold drawing-room done by the local upholsterer is atrociously vulgar, but the cathedral of Puebla is not. Gold—polished, glittering, shameless gold—blazes down and up and across at one; from the stone rosettes in the vaulting overhead, from the grilles in front of the chapels, from the railings between which the priests walk to altar and choir, from the onyx pulpit and the barricade of gigantic candlesticks in front of the altar, from the altar itself —one of those carefully insane eighteenth-century affairs, in which a frankly pagan tiempolito and great lumps of Christian symbolism have become

47

gloriously muddled for all time. Gold flashes in the long straight sun shafts overhead, twinkles in the candle flames, glitters from the censers and the chains of the censers. The back of the priest at the altar is incrusted with gold, and to-day—for Christmas lingers—all the pillars from capital to base are swathed in the finest of crimson velvet, fringed with gold. It isn't vulgar, it isn't even gaudy. It has surpassed all that and has entered into the realm of the bewildering—the flabber-gastric.

As I sank upon one of the sparsely occupied benches " para los señores," there was exhaled from the organ, somewhere behind and above me, a dozen or more bars of Chopin. During the many sartorial interims of the mass the organ coquetted frequently with Chopin as well as with Saint-Saëns, Massenet, and Gounod in some of his less popular but as successfully cloying moments—and never anywhere have I seen so much incense. As a rule, unless one sits well forward in churches, the incense only tantalizes. Swing and jerk as the little boys may, it persists in clinging to the altar and the priests, in being sucked into the draught of the candle flames and then floating up to the sunlight of the dome. It rarely reaches the populace until it has become cool and thin. At Puebla they may be more prodigal of it, or they may use a different kind. It at any rate belches out at one in fat, satiating clouds of pearl-gray and sea-blue, and what with Chopin and all the little gasping flames, the rich, deliberate, incrusted group about the altar, the forest of crimson pillars and the surfeit of gold, I experienced one of those agreeable, harmless, ecclesiastical debauches that in Mexico, where the apparatus of worship does not often rise above the tawdry, and the music is almost always execrable, are perforce rare.

Toward the end of it, the central and most splendid figure among those at the altar turned to execute some symbolic gesture and I recognized his grace, the Bishop. More than half incrusted with gold and, for the rest, swathed in white lace over purple, he was far more splendid than when, two years before, he had confirmed my godchild Geronimo, son of Felipe, in the weatherworn church at Mizantla. But he was none the less the same poisonous-looking old body with whom on that occasion I had had " words." I recognized, among other things, his fat, overhanging underlip. By its own weight it fell outward from his lower teeth, turned half about and disclosed a rubbery in-

49

side that, with its blue veins against a background of congested red, had reminded me, I remember, of a piece of German fancy-work. Undoubtedly it was his grace on a visit to a neighboring see and officiating through the courtesy of a brother bishop in the great cathedral.

Strange, I thought, that such a looking old person should be associated in my mind with so pretty an incident and so springlike a day. For the sight of him took me back, as the saying is, to a hot, radiant February morning when the sun blazed down upon the ranch for the first time in two weeks and I had ridden into the village to have Geronimo, a charming child of six, confirmed. There was the inevitable Mexican delay in starting, while horses and mules fled around the pasture refusing to be caught, while the cook made out " la lista "—three cents worth of this and six cents worth of that—while mislaid tenates were found, provided with string handles and hung over pommels. But we staggered off at last—Felipe leading on foot with a sky-blue bundle under one arm (it was a clean pair of trousers) and his loose white drawers rolled up to his thighs. I wondered why, on this great occasion, he did not wear the neckerchief of mauve silk we had given him at Christmas until a moment later I discovered it in two pieces around the necks of his wife and Geronimo. His wife followed him on a horse, and Geronimo, astride at her back, clutched at her waist with one hand and with the other attempted most of the way in to prevent his cartwheel of a hat from bumping against his mother's shoulder blades in front and falling off behind. Then a San Juan Indian in fluttering white, bearing on his back Felipe's sick baby in a basket, pattered along over the mudholes with the aid of a staff. Trinidad, the mayordomo, followed next on his horse, and I came last on a mule, from where I could see the others vanishing one by one into the shady jungle, scrambling below me down wet, rocky hillsides and stringing through the hot pastures full of damp, sweet vapors and hidden birds that paused and listened to their own languid voices.

The river was high and swift after the rain, and for those who counted on another's legs to get them across, there was the interminable three or four minutes when one takes a reef in one's own, unconditionally surrenders to the steed, tries not to look down at the water, and with a pinched smile at the opposite shore reflects that: " If the beast keeps three or even two of his little hoofs on the

stones at the same time until we reach the sand
bar—how trivial! But if he doesn't he will go
swirling downstream like an empty barrel, my head
will smash against the first boulder, and it will
all be very sad."

The bishop's advent had, if not quite the importance of a fiesta, at least the enlivening qualities
of a fiestita. There was so much movement and
talk and color in the drowsy town, and so many
drunken Indians shook hands with me and patted
me on the back, that if it had not been Thursday,
I should have known it was Sunday. The bishop
had not been to Mizantla for some said five and
others eight years. But in either period it seems
that unconfirmed children pile up amazingly.
Grouped about the weed-grown open space on the
church's shady side there were almost four hundred of them, not including parents and godparents,
and this was the second of the three days' opportunity.

But there was the same vagueness as to when
the ceremony would begin that there had been about
the date of the previous visit. Some, remembering
perhaps that most gringos have an inscrutable
prejudice in favor of the definite, courteously named
an hour—any hour; two, five, half past six. Others

recalled that evening was the time, while a few assured me the bishop had come and gone the day before. Nobody, however, seemed to care, and I asked myself as Felipe and Geronimo and I sat on a crumbling parapet and watched the bright colored crowd: "Why should I care? What difference does it make whether I sit here in the shade or in the shade at the ranch?"

But at last there began to be a slow activity —a going in and a coming out at the door of the priest's house. I watched people go in empty-handed and come out with a slip of paper in one hand and a long yellow candle in the other. The slip of paper left me cold, but the tapering yellow candle mystically called. In Jalapa I had often stood for an hour staring at the moderate revolutions of the great hoop on which the pendent wicks grow fatter and fatter as the velero patiently bathes them in boiling tallow, and I had yearned to possess one. Yet, heretofore, I had denied myself; the desire, it seemed to me, was like that craving for heirlooms and ancestors on the part of persons to whom such innocent sensualities have been cruelly denied. To-day, however, long virtue was to have a short, vicarious reward, for Geronimo's little soul was at the moment entirely in my hands, and it was but proper that his way to heaven should be lighted by a blessed candle. So when I came out of the priest's house I, too, had one (" Bang! went saxpence ") as well as the " certificate of confirmation " (" Bang! " went another), on which was written my godchild's name, and the names of his parents and my name. It took hours for everyone to be supplied, but they were as nothing compared to the hours we waited in the church for the bishop. Except in front of the altar, the nave had been fenced off by a continuous line of benches facing inward, and on these the children stood with their sponsors behind them. Like most Mexican children, their behavior was admirable. They rarely cry, they rarely quarrel, and their capacity for amusing themselves with nothing is without limit. Had I the ordering of this strange, unhappy world, I think all children would be born Mexican and remain so until they were fifteen.

That they in a measure outgrow their youthful serenity, however, seemed to be proved by exhausted relatives all about me who, after the first hour of waiting, began to roll their eyes when they met mine and dispatch a succession of Sister Annes to peer through the windows of the priest's sala. " Está dormiendo " (he is sleeping), in a hoarse whisper, was repeated so often that—my breakfast had been a cup of chocolate and a cigarette—the hinges in my knees began to work both ways, and just outside the church door I recklessly bought and ate something (it cauterized me as it went down) wrapped in a tortilla. When I returned, the bishop, with three priests behind him, was standing at the top of the altar steps. He was wearing his miter and the tips of his fingers lightly touched one another, as a bishop's fingers should, on the apex of his stomach. It was a thrilling moment.

Then, combining, in a quite wonderful fashion, extreme rapidity with an air of ecclesiastical calm, he made his confirmatory way down one side of the nave, across the end, and up the other, preceded by one priest and followed by two. The first gathered up the certificates (no laying on of hands unless one has paid one's twenty-five centavos) and read the name of the child next in line to the bishop, who murmured the appropriate formula, made a tiny sign of the cross on a tiny forehead with the end of a large, dirty thumb, and moved on. The second, with a bit of absorbent cotton dipped in oil, swabbed the spot on which the cross had been signed, while the third, taking advantage of the

55

general rapture, gently relieved everyone of his blessed candle (it had never been lighted) and carried it away to be sold again.

But by the time the first priest reached my family party he had grown tired and careless. Instead of collecting the certificates singly, he began to take them in twos and threes with the result that they became mixed, and Geronimo was confirmed, not as Geronimo, but as " Saturnina," which happened to be the name of the little snubnosed Totonac girl standing next to him. When I realized what had happened, I protested. Whereupon his grace and I proceeded to have "words." With exceeding bitterness he then reperformed the rite, and if the eyes of the first priest could have killed, I should have withered on my slender stalk. The priest with the cotton also sought to annihilate me with an undertoned remark to the effect that my conduct was a " barbaridad," but the third was not only sinpatico—he was farther away from the bishop. As, with much tenderness, he disengaged Geronimo's reluctant fingers from the candle, he severely looked at me and winked.

Then we wandered down to the shabby little plaza, where I bought Geronimo some toys and Felipe wanted to buy me a drink. But as Felipe

was still looking prematurely old as the result of
something suspiciously like delirium tremens a few
weeks before, I sanctimoniously declined and bade
them good-by.

There is no twilight in those tropics, and before the mayordomo and I reached home, darkness gathered in the deep valley, crept behind us
up the mountainside, and all at once, as they say
in Spanish, " it nighted." It was impossible to see
the trail or even the sky, and we lurched on and on
as through an interminable world of black velvet.
Most of the way I kept my eyes shut—crouching
down on the pommel to escape overhanging vines
and the terrible outstretched fingers of mala mujer.
Twice we lost our hats, and once my mule stuck
deep and fast in the mud until we jumped into it
ourselves and pulled him out. On this road after
dark it is usually difficult to think of anything except that in a little while one's neck will be broken;
but that evening, with my eyelids squeezed together and my feet prudently hanging free of the
stirrups, I kept recalling Felipe's clumsy, charming
devotion to his ethereal little son and the satisfaction he had unconsciously displayed when Geronimo
toddled out of the church—confirmed.

Although Felipe gets frightfully drunk, neglects

his wife for other women, and regards a machete as the most convincing form of argument, he has excellent qualities; but I shouldn't think of him as religious exactly. And yet—and yet—Felipe and his wife are really married (it seems rather snobbish of them, but it's a fact), and from the knowledge that his children have been baptized by the priest and confirmed by the bishop, he gets some sort of an agreeable sensation.

VI

WHY people are what they are is always an interesting subject on which to exert one's talents, however slight, for observation and inference. On an isolated Mexican farm one spends many odd moments in considering and attempting to explain the traits of the people who condescend to work for one. For most of the problems of one's daily life there arise from those traits, and by them, all are complicated. The amicable relations between employer and employed everywhere is one that necessitates on the former's part considerable tact to preserve, but in Mexico both the nation's history and the people's temperament combine to render the situation one of unusual delicacy.

In 1519 Spain and the Roman Catholic Church affixed themselves to Mexico's throat and were with extreme difficulty detached from it only after three hundred years. During most of that time, in addition to the fact that the Church got possession actually of something more than a third of the country's entire property, " real, personal, and mixed," the metaphorical expression, " he could not call his soul his own," was true of the inhabitants in its baldest, its most literal sense. To call one's soul one's own in Mexico between the years 1527 and 1820 was to be tried in secret by the Holy Office of the Inquisition and then turned over to the secular authorities—a formality that deceived no one—to be either publicly strangled and then burned, or burned without even the preliminary solace of strangulation. " The principal crimes of which the Holy Office took cognizance," we read, " were heresy, sorcery, withcraft, polygamy, seduction, imposture, and personation "—a tolerably elastic category. Without the slightest difficulty it could be stretched to cover anyone " not in sympathy with the work," and during the period in which the Holy Office was exercised it covered many.

It is true the royal order by which the Inquisition was formally established in Mexico exempted Indians from its jurisdiction, but when the clause was observed—which it was not in the case of Indians who displayed a capacity for thought—it was almost the only form of oppression from which, under the bigoted and avaricious rule of Spain, they were exempt. Until the advent of the conquerors this part of the new world had been, for no one knows how long, a slaughterhouse of the gods. Spain and the Church continued a carnage of their own in the name of God.

The limited scope of these impressions permits of scarcely a reference to Mexico's history. I can only assert that almost every phase of it is imbedded in layer upon layer· of the rottenest type of ecclesiastical politics and that the great mass of the people to-day reflects—in a fashion curiously modified at unexpected moments by the national awakening—its generations of mental and physical subjection. For whatever, from time to time, has happened to be the form of government, the people have never enjoyed any large measure of freedom. Even now, with an acute, patriotic, and enlightened president at the head of the nation, Mexico—and quite inevitably—is not a republic, but a military Diazpotism.

In the name of gods and of God, of kings, dictators, popes, generals, emperors, and presidents, the people of Mexico have been treated, one would be inclined to say, like so many head of irresponsible cattle, if cattle, as a rule, were not treated more solicitously. And this general tendency of the governor toward the governed has accentuated certain traits easy enough to isolate and describe, if they were not complicated by the facts that: First, the Mexican of to-day naturally has many characteristics in common with the Spaniard who begat him and whom he still hates; second, that the nation is becoming more and more conscious of itself as a nation, and, third, that in a multitude of petty ways a kind of mediæval tyranny is still often exercised by the very persons who, as officials of a theoretically excellent republic, ought to stand for all that is liberal and just.

Now, if the attitude of a Mexican peon were always consistently that of the oppressed and patient creature who looks upon his patrón as omnipotent and omniscient, or if it were always that of the highfalutin Spaniard whom at times he so much resembles—or, if it were always that of Young Mexico, conscious of at least his theoretical independence and in theory " as good as anybody," there would be little difficulty in getting along with him; one would know at any given moment how to treat him. But as a matter of fact it is a rather intricate combination of all three, and one can rarely predict which he will choose to exhibit. Add to this an incredible depth of superstition that is both innate and very carefully encouraged by the Church, and it is not difficult to see why an employer in certain parts of Mexico is compelled to treat his laborers much as one has to treat nervous and unreasonable children.

Although they are hired and receive wages on various terms of agreement, the normal relation between the proprietor of, say, a café finca of moderate size and the people who work for him, suggests in many respects the relation that existed before the Civil War between our Southerners of the better type and their slaves. Some of the people have small farms of their own in the neigborhood, but when they go to work for any length of time they usually close their houses and live on the ranch of their employer in one-roomed huts built by the patrón at a cost—if they are made of bamboo— of from six to ten dollars an edifice. Closing their houses for the coffee-picking season consists of gathering up four or five primitive pottery cooking utensils, several babies, a pair of thin and faded sarapes, calling to the dogs and strolling out of the door. Under ordinary amicable circumstances they are disposed to look up to the patrón, to be flattered by his notice of them—to regard him, in fact, as of different and finer clay than themselves. And when this lowly and dependent mood is upon them there is not only nothing the señor cannot, in their opinion, accomplish if he desires to—there are no demands upon his time, his money, his implements, and his sympathies that they hesitate to make. The proprietor of a far-away ranch acquires a certain proficiency in the performance of almost every kindly office, from obstetrics to closing the eyes of the dead.

One Agapito, whose baby died on our place, informed us—after we had sufficiently condoled and he had cheerfully assured us that the baby was "better off with God"—that it would give him and his wife great pleasure to pay us the compliment of having the wake in our sala! There, of course, was a delicate situation at once. Agapito yearned for the prestige that would be his if we permitted him to suspend his dead baby—dressed in mosquito netting and orange blossoms—against the sala wall and leave it there to the edification of the countryside for a day and a night. To refuse was, without doubt, to offend him; but to consent was to establish a somewhat ghastly precedent impossible in subsequent cases of affliction to ignore. As my brother declared, when we withdrew to discuss the matter, one had to choose between hurting Agapito's feelings and turning the sala into a perpetual morgue. Agapito was in several respects an efficient and valuable person. He could even persuade the machine for dispulping coffee-berries to work smoothly when—as they express it—" it does not wish to." But, nevertheless, with much regret we decided to hurt Agapito's feelings. Like children they do not shrink from making naïvely preposterous demands upon one, and like children their sense of obligation is almost entirely lacking. They are given to bringing one presents of oranges and bananas, or inedible blood puddings and cakes when they kill a pig or have a party, but they are rarely incited to display appreciation of kindness—even when it would be easy for them to do so—in a way that counts.

One afternoon, during the busiest season of the year on a coffee ranch, all the coffee-pickers—men, women, and children—with the exception of one family, suddenly struck. When asked what the trouble was, the spokesman in a florid and pompous address declared that they were " all brothers and must pick together or not at all." It came out during the interview that the father of the family who had not struck had received permission for himself, his wife, and six small children to pick in a block of coffee by themselves, and to this the others had been induced to object. Why they objected they could not say, because they did not know. It was explained to them that the man had wished his family to work apart for the sole and sensible reason that, first, he and his wife could take better care of the children when they were not scattered among the crowd, and, secondly, that as the trees of the particular block he had asked to be allowed to pick in were younger and smaller than the others, the children had less difficulty in reaching the branches. He not only derived no financial advantage from the change, he was voluntarily making some sacrifice by going to pick where the coffee, owing to the youth of the trees, was less abundant.

"Don't you see that this is the truth and all there is to it?" the strikers were asked.

"Yes."

"And now that it has been explained, won't you go back to work?"

"No."

"But why not?"

"Because."

"Because what?"

"Because we must all pick together."

A strike for higher wages or shorter hours or more and better food is usual and always comprehensible anywhere, but one has to go to Mexico, I imagine, to experience a strike that involves neither

66

a question of material advantage nor of abstract principle. It was recalled to them that the fact of their being " all brothers " did not operate against their eloping with one another's wives and slashing one another with machetes in the mazy dance whenever they felt so inclined—a reflection that produced much merriment, especially among the ladies. But upon the point at issue it had no effect whatever, and irritating as it was to be forced into submitting to this sort of thing, before work could be resumed the family of eight had to be sent for and told to pick with the others. All these people were indebted to their employer for loans, for medicines—for assistance of various kinds too numerous to mention or to remember, and, in their way, they liked him and liked the ranch. I can account for such inconsiderate imbecility only by supposing that after generations of oppression the desire among an ignorant and emotional people to assert their independence in small matters becomes irresistible from time to time, even when they cannot discover that their rights have been in any way infringed upon.

However, their rights *are* constantly infringed upon in the most obvious and brazen manner, and knowledge of this undoubtedly contributes to their uncomfortable habit of vibrating between an attitude of doglike trust and one of the most exaggerated suspicion. Last year, for example, a stone bridge was being built in a small town some six or eight miles away from our ranch. As the heavy summer rains were but a few months off, it was desirable that the bridge should be completed. Labor, however, was exceedingly scarce, and for a long time the work made no visible progress. At first the authorities resorted to the usual plan of making arrests for drunkenness and obliging the victims to haul stones and mortar, but as this immediately resulted in the exercise of unusual self-restraint on the part of the populace, the jefe político evolved the quaint conceit of detaining every able-bodied man who appeared in town without trousers! The Indians in that part of the country, and many of the people who are not pure Indian, wear, instead of the skin-tight Mexican trousers, a pair of long, loose white cotton drawers resembling in cut and fit the lower part of a suit of pajamas. They are not only a perfectly respectable garment, they are vastly more practical and comfortable than the pantalones, inasmuch as they can be rolled above the knee and, in a land of mud and streams, kept clean and dry. But until the jefe had acquired a force sufficient to complete the bridge, he arrested everybody who wore them. A law had been passed, he said, declaring them to be indecent. Just when the law had been passed and by whom he did not trouble to explain. Among the small rancheros of the neighborhood who did not own a pair of trousers, the edict caused not only inconvenience but now and then positive hardship. Many of them who had not heard of it and innocently attended church or market were sent to bridge-building for indefinite periods when they ought to have been at home harvesting their corn. Their crops were either spoiled or stolen. The Indians on our place did not dare venture into town for supplies until we bought a pair of trousers for lending purposes. "Trinidad (or Lucio, or Jesús) is going to town and begs that you will do him the favor of lending him the pants," was an almost daily request for weeks.[1]

---

[1] Since I wrote the above, the following item of news appeared in the *Mexican Herald* of February 11, 1908:

FORCED TO WEAR TROUSERS

MOUNTAINEERS AROUND GUANAJUATO

PREFER TO PAY FINES.

Special Dispatch to the *Herald*.

GUANAJUATO, February 10th.—The local treasury will soon be full to overflowing from the numerous fines collected from sons of the

VIVA MEXICO!

I remember one jefe político to whom it occurred
that he might start a butcher shop and ruin the
business of the only ˙other butcher shop in town,
which was kept by a man he happened to dislike.
When he had completed his arrangements for the
sale of meat, he caused a rumor to circulate among
the lower classes to the effect that life would be
a gladder, sweeter thing for all concerned if the
meat he was now prepared to dispense should find
a market both ready and sustained. To the American and English rancheros of the neighborhod he
had letters written by various friends of his who
happened to know them; courteous not to say
punctilious letters that, however, contained somewhere between the lines an ominous rumble. " I
thought it might interest you to learn that H—,
the jefe, has opened a butcher shop and would consider it an honor if you were to favor him with your
patronage, instead of bestowing it upon his com-
petitor," the letters ran in part. Though somewhat more rhetorical, it all sounded to the un-

---

mountains who daily endeavor to enter this ancient town clad in cotton
drawers.   The law is strict in this particular, and the police in the
suburbs have strict orders to see that no peon enters the town without
a pair of factory-made trousers.

[It would be interesting to know who, in Guanajuato, owns the
largest interest in the local trousers factory.]

attuned ear as innocent as any of the numerous advertisements one receives by post in the course of a week at home. But it wasn't. In a " republic," where the governors of the various states must be without question the political friends of the president, and the jefes are usually, with no more question, the political friends of the governors, the suggestion that a jefe would not object to one's purchasing beefsteaks from him is not lightly to be ignored. The local jefe can, in a hundred subtle ways, make one's residence in Mexico extremely difficult and disagreeable. Every foreigner who received one of the inspired epistles changed his butcher the next day. Another jefe of my acquaintance—a rather charming man—decided to pave a certain country road chiefly because it went through some land owned by his brother. As most of the able-bodied convicts of that district were engaged in paving a much more important highway and he could not very well draw upon their forces, he magnificently sent out a messenger who floundered through the mud from ranch to ranch, announcing to the countryside that henceforth every man would have to labor, without compensation, one day in eight upon the road. Now, to most of the people who received the message, this particular road was of no importance; they rarely used it and they owned no land through which it ran. And yet— whether from the habit of submitting to tyranny, or from guilty consciences, I don't know—many responded with their time and their toil. When asked, as we frequently were, for advice on the subject, we refrained from giving any.

The habit of suspicion and the impulse to make, for no very definite reason, little displays of personal independence would tax one's patience and amiability to the utmost if one did not keep on hand a reserve fund of these qualities with which to fortify oneself against frequent exhibitions of Mexican honor. In referring to this somewhat rococo subject, it is perhaps but fair for me to admit that even so comparatively simple a matter as the Anglo-Saxon sense of honor presents certain difficulties to my understanding. Explain and expound as many intelligent gentlemen have to me, for instance, I have never been able to grasp why it is so much more dishonorable to evade one's gambling debts than it is to evade one's laundress. Therefore I do not feel competent to throw a great light upon the kind of honor that obtains in Mexico. I can only observe that, like politeness, smallpox, and fine weather, it is very prevalent, and record an example or two of the many that arise in my memory, by way of illustrating one of the obstacles in the employer's path.

A few winters ago we hired a youth to bring our letters and fresh meat every day from the town to the ranch. He performed this monotonous service with commendable regularity, and with a regularity not so commendable always cut off at least a quarter of the meat after leaving the butcher shop and gave it to his mother who lived in town. Futhermore, when the workmen on the place intrusted him with letters to post on his return, he posted them if they were stamped, but scattered them in fragments if they were not, and pocketed the money. We knew he did both these things because we found and identified some of the epistolary fragments, and his mother had the monumental brass to complain to the butcher when the meat was tough! But even so, he was a convenience—none of the laborers could be regularly spared at the time—and we made no moan. One day, however, it was impossible to ignore the matter; he arrived with a bit of beefsteak about as large as a mutton chop and had the effrontery, as we thought, to deliver it without a word of explanation. So, as the imposition had been going on for at least six weeks,

73

he was as kindly as possible, most unfortunately, accused. Then followed an exhibition of outraged innocence such as I have never before seen. He turned a kind of Nile green; he clenched his fist and beat upon his chest. He made an impassioned address in which he declared that, although his family was poor and needed the twenty-five centavos a day we paid him, he could not continue to work for anyone who had sought to cast a reflection upon his spotless honor; and he ended by bursting into tears and sobbing for ten minutes with his head on a bag of coffee.

The tragic, humorous, and altogether grotesque part of the affair was that on this particular day for the first time, no doubt, since we had employed him, he *hadn't* stolen the meat! We learned from the butcher a few hours afterwards that there had been scarcely any beefsteak in the shop when the boy had called, but that he had sent a few ounces, thinking it was better than nothing at all. We lost our messenger; his mother would not allow him to work for persons who doubted his honesty.

A friend of mine had in his employ an old man —an ex-bullfighter—who took care of the horses and accompanied the various members of the family when they went for a ride. He was given to gambling, and on one occasion when he had lost all his money but could not bring himself to leave the game, he gambled away a saddle and bridle of his employer. Shortly afterwards my friend recognized them in the window of a harness shop and bought them back, without, however, mentioning the fact to old Preciliano, who, when casually asked where they were, replied quite as casually that at the public stable where the horses were kept they had become mixed with some other equipment and taken away by mistake. He explained that he knew the distant ranchero who had inadvertently done this and that steps had been taken to have them returned. For several weeks my friend amused himself by asking for—and getting—minute details of the saddle's whereabouts and the probable date of its arrival, and then one day he abruptly accused Preciliano of having lost it in a game of cards.

This was followed by almost exactly a repetition of the performance we had been given by the meat-and-letter boy. Preciliano was not only astonished that the señor could for a moment imagine such a thing, he was hurt—wounded—cruelly smitten in his old age by the hand he had never seen raised except in kindness. All was lost save honor. That, thank God, he could still retain—but not there; not under that roof. He could not remain covered with shame in the shadow of so hideous a suspicion. Honor demanded that he should "separate" himself at once—honor demanded all sorts of things in this vein until my friend, who said he was positively beginning to believe Preciliano very much as Preciliano believed himself, suddenly stooped down and pulled the saddle and bridle from under the table. Collapse. Tears. Forgiveness. Tableau.

Preciliano subsequently left this family—gave up an agreeable and lucrative position—because the wife of the employer thoughtfully suggested that, on account of his advancing years, it would be wiser of him not to exercise a certain imperfectly broken horse. He was "covered with shame" and sorrowfully bade them farewell.

VII

HERE is a letter from a coffee plantation:
When I got back in October, they received me with formalities—gave me a kind
of Roman triumph. If it hadn't been so pathetic I
should have laughed; if it hadn't been so funny I
should have cried. For I had been fourteen hours
on a slow-climbing mule, and you know—or rather
you don't know—how the last interminable two
hours of that kind of riding unstrings one. Being
Mexican, everything about the Roman triumph
went wrong and fell perfectly flat. In the first
place they expected me a day earlier, and when I
didn't arrive they decided—Heaven knows why—
that I wouldn't come the next day, but the day
after. In the meanwhile I appeared late in the
afternoon of the day between. They had built in
front of the piazza a wobbly arch of great glossy
leaves and red flowers, and from post to post had
hung chains of red, white, and green tissue paper.
But the arch, of course, had blown down in the
night and most of the paper garlands had been

rained on and were hanging limply to the posts. All this, they assured me, would have been repaired had I arrived a day later, and I marveled at my self-control as I enthusiastically admired the beauty of a welcoming arch lying prostrate in the mud.

It had been the pleasant intention of everyone to assemble and welcome me home, and when at the entrance to the ranch the Indian who lives there gave a prolonged, falsetto cry (un grito)—the signal agreed on—and I rode up the slope to the clanging of the bell we ring to call in the pickers, and the detonations of those terrible Mexican rockets that give no light but rend the sky apart, I had a feeling as of a concourse awaiting me. The concourse, however, had given me up until the next day, and when I got off my mule I found that the entire festivities were being conducted by Manuel the house-boy, Rosalía the cook, and Trinidad the mayordomo. Trinidad shot off all six cartridges in his revolver and then shook hands with me. Rosalía was attached to the bell rope—Manuel was manipulating the rockets. At that moment I knew exactly how the hero feels when the peasantry (no doubt such plays are now extinct) exclaims: " The young squire comes of age to-day. Hurray, hurray, hurray! There will be great doings up at the hall. Hurray, hurray, hurray!" It was all so well meant that when I went into my bedroom I could not bring myself to scold at what I found there. On the clean, brown cedar walls they had pasted pictures—advertisements of sewing machines and breakfast foods and automobiles, cut from the back pages of magazines and slapped on anywhere. They see but few pictures, and ours, although rather meaningless to them, are fascinating. A picture is a picture, and my walls were covered with them; but I pretended to be greatly pleased. Since then I have been quietly soaking them off at the tactful rate of about two a week.

Trinidad, the new mayordomo, seems to have done well in my absence. He planted thirty-five thousand new coffee trees with an intelligence positively human. Casimiro, his predecessor, and I parted last year—not in anger, only in sorrow. Casimiro had been a highwayman—a bandit. His police record, they say, makes creepy reading on dark and windy nights. That, however, I never took in consideration. It was only when he began to gamble and to make good his losses by selling me my own corn and pocketing the money that we bade each other good-by. There was no scene. When I told him such things could not go on, he gravely agreed with me that they couldn't, and without resentment departed the next morning. They are strange people. When they do lose control of themselves they go to any lengths; there is likely to be a scene more than worth the price of admission. Somebody usually gets killed. But nothing short of this would seem to be, as a rule, worth while, and on the surface their manner is one of indifference—detachment. Trinidad, who took Casimiro's place, rose, so to speak, from the ranks. He was an arriero for seven years and then drifted here as a day laborer. But he understands coffee, and the experiment of suddenly placing him over all the others has so far been a success.

What a watchful eye the authorities keep on them even in far-away places like this! The instant Trinidad ceased to be a common laborer on whatever he could earn a day by picking coffee, hauling firewood, cleaning the trees, and received a salary of thirty-five pesos a month, his taxes were raised. They all pay a monthly tax (the " contribución " it is called) of a few centavos, although what most of them, owning absolutely nothing, are taxed for, it would be hard to say, unless it be for breathing the air of heaven—for being alive at all. He tried to keep secret the fact of his advancement, but it became known of course, and his tax, to his great disgust, was raised fifteen or twenty cents.

Last week we had our first picking of the year and, weather permitting (which it won't be), we shall pick with more or less continuity for the next four months. Coffee is different from other crops ("not like other girls") and often inclines me to believe it has acquired some of its characteristics from prolonged and intimate contact with the hands that pick it. For quite in the Mexican manner it cannot bring itself to do anything so definite and thorough as to ripen—like wheat or corn or potatoes —all at once. A few berries turn red on every tree and have to be removed before they fall off. By the time this has been done from one end of the place to the other, more have ripened and reddened and the pickers begin again. "Poco á poco—not to-day shall we be ready for you, but to-morrow, or perhaps next week. To do anything so final— in fact, to be ready on any specific date is not the custom of the country," the trees seem to say. However, it is just as well. Nature apparently knew what she was doing. To pick the berries properly requires skill and time, and if they all ripened at once one could not take care of them.

Beyond the fact that you "don't take sugar, thank you," and like to have the cream poured in first, do you know anything about coffee? Did you know that the pretty, fussy trees (they are really more like large shrubs) won't grow in the sun and won't grow in the shade, but have to be given companionship in the form of other trees that, high above them, permit just enough and not too much sunlight to filter mildly in? And that unless you twist off the berries in a persuasive, almost gentle fashion, you so hurt their feelings that in the spring they may refuse to flower? And that the branches are so brittle, they have a way of cracking off from the weight of their own crop? And that wherever there is coffee there is also a tough, graceful little vine about as thick as a telegraph wire which, if left uncut, winds itself around and around a tree, finally strangling it to death as a snake strangles a rabbit?

When I see the brown hands of the pickers fluttering like nimble birds among the branches, and think of the eight patient processes to which the little berries must be subjected before they can become a cup of drinkable coffee, I often wonder how and by whom their secret was wrested from them. Was it an accident like the original whitening of sugar, when—so we used to be told—a chicken with clay on its feet ran over a mound of crude, brown crystals? Or did a dejected Arabian, having heard all his life that (like the tomato of our grand-mothers') it was a deadly thing, attempt by drinking it to assuage forever a hopeless passion for some bulbul of the desert, and then find himself not dead, but waking? A careless woman drops a bottle of bluing into a vat of wood pulp and lo! for the first time we have colored writing paper. But no one ever inadvertently picked, dispulped, fermented, washed, dried, hulled, roasted, ground, and boiled coffee, and unless most of these things are done to it, it is of no possible use.

After the coffee is picked it is brought home in sacks, measured, and run through the dispulper, a machine that removes the tough red, outer skin. Every berry (except the pea berry—a freak) is composed of two beans, and these are covered with a sweet, slimy substance known as the " honey," which has to ferment and rot before the beans may be washed. Washing simply removes the honey and those pieces of the outer skin that have escaped the teeth of the machine and flowed from the front end where they weren't wanted. Four or five changes of water are made in the course of the operation, and toward the last, when the rotted honey has been washed away, leaving the beans hard and clean in their coverings of parchment, one of the men takes off his trousers, rolls up his drawers, and knee deep in the heavy mixture of coffee and water drags his feet as rapidly as he can around the cement washing tank until the whole mass is in motion with a swirling eddy in the center. Into the eddy gravitate all the impurities—the foreign substances—the dead leaves and twigs and unwelcome hulls, and when they all seem to be there, the man deftly scoops them up with his hands and tosses them over the side. Then, if it be a fine hot day, the soggy mess is shoveled on the asoleadero (literally, the sunning place), an immense sloping stone platform covered with smooth cement, and there it is spread out to dry while men in their bare feet constantly turn it over with wooden hoes in order that the beans may receive the sun equally on all sides.

It sounds simple, and if one numbered among one's employees a Joshua who could command the sun to stand still when one wished it to, it doubtless would be. But no matter how much coffee there may be spread out on the asoleadero, the sun not only loses its force at a certain hour and then inconsiderately sets, it sometimes refuses for weeks at a time to show itself at all. During these dreary eternities the half-dried coffee is stowed away in sacks or, when it is too wet to dispose of in this manner without danger of molding, it is heaped up in ridges on the asoleadero and covered. When it rains, work of all kinds in connection with the coffee necessarily ceases. The dryers cannot dry and the pickers cannot pick. Even when it is not actually raining the pickers won't go out if the trees are still wet. For the water from the shaken branches chills and stiffens their bloodless hands and soaks through their cotton clothes to the skin. If one's plantation and one's annual crop are large enough to justify the expense, one may defy the sun by investing in what is known as a secadero— a machine for drying coffee by artificial heat. But I haven't arrived at one of these two-thousand-dollar sun-scorners—yet.

That is as far as I go with my coffee—I pick it, dispulp it, wash it, dry it, and sell it. But while the first four of these performances sometimes bid fair to worry me into my grave before my prime, and the fourth at least is of vital importance, as the flavor of coffee may certainly be marred, if not made, in the drying, they are but the prelude

to what is eventually done to it before you criti-
cally sip it and declare it to be good or bad. Wom-
en and children pick it over by hand, separating it
into different classes; it is then run through one
machine that divests it of its parchment covering;
another, with the uncanny precision of mindless
things, gropes for beans that happen to be of exactly
the same shape, wonderfully finds them, and drops
them into their respective places; while at the same
time it is throwing out every bean that either nature
or the dispulping machine has in the slightest degree mutilated. The sensitiveness and apperception
of this iron and wooden box far exceed my own.
Often I am unable to see the difference between
the beans it has chosen to disgorge into one sack
and the beans it has relegated to another—to feel
the justice of its irrevocable decisions. But they
are always just, and every bean it drops into the
defective sack will be found, on examination, to
be defective. Then there is still another machine
for polishing the bean—rubbing off the delicate,
tissue-paper membrane that covers it inside of the
parchment. This process does not affect the flavor.
In fact nothing affects the flavor of coffee after it
has once been dried; but the separation and the
polishing give it what is known to the trade as

" style." And in the trade there is as much poppy-
cock about coffee as there is about wine and cigars.
When you telephone to your grocer for a mixture
of Mocha and Java do you by any chance imagine
that you are going to receive coffee from Arabia
and the Dutch islands? What you do receive, the
coffee kings alone know. There are, I have been
told, a few sacks of real Mocha in the United
States, just as there are a few real Vandykes and
Holbeins, and if you are very lucky indeed, the
Mocha in your mixture will have been grown in
Mexico.

Sometimes at the height of the picking season
the day is not long enough, the washing tanks are
not large enough, and the workers are not numerous
enough to attend to both the coffee-drying on the
asoleadero and the growing pile of berries that are
constantly being carried in from the trees. When
this happens the dispulping has to be done at night,
and until four or five in the morning the monotonous plaint of the machine, grinding, grinding
like the mills of some insatiable Mexican god,
comes faintly over from the tanks. Under a flaring
torch and fortified with a bottle of aguardiente the
men take turns through the long night at filling
the hopper and turning the heavy wheel, bursting

now and then into wild, improvised recitatives that
are answered by whomever happens for the moment to be most illuminated by either the aguardiente or the divine fire. They begin to improvise
to this rapid, savage burst of a few minor phrases
from the time they are children. Almost any grown
man can do it, although there is a standard of excellence in the art (I have begun to detect it when
I hear it), recognized among themselves, that only
a few attain. It takes into consideration both the
singer's gift for dramatic or lyric invention and the
quality of his voice, a loud, strained tenor with
falsetto embellishments being the most desirable. I
have heard Censio, the mayordomo's little boy,
aged three or four, singing, for an hour at a time,
sincere and simple eulogies of his father's cows.
Since I brought him a small patrol wagon drawn
by two spirited iron horses his voice, however, is no
longer lifted in commemoration of " O mis vacas!
O mis vacas! O mis vacas! " but of " O mis caballitos! O mis caballitos! O mis caballitos! " They
improvise, too, at the dances, where the music is
usually a harp and a jarana—breaking in anywhere,
saying their say, and then waiting for the reply.
Women rarely take part in these Tannhäuseresque
diversions, although I remember one woman at a

dance on my own piazza who got up and proceeded
to chant with a wealth of personal and rather embarrassing detail the story of her recent desertion
by the man she loved. He had of course deserted
her for some one else, and at the end of her remarkable narrative she sang, in a perfect debauch
of emotion and self-pity: "But I am of a forgiving
nature! Come back, come back, my rose, my heart,
my soul—the bed is big enough for three!" Sometimes when there is a dance at a neighboring ranch
the harpist and his son, who plays the jarana, stop
at my place on their way home in the morning
and play to me (the son also improvises) while I
am at breakfast. The harpist is always drunk, and
his instrument, after a night of hard work, out of
tune. He appeared not long ago when I had staying with me a Boston lawyer—my only visitor so
far this year.

"Isn't it horrible to eat soft boiled eggs and
toast in this pandemonium," I called to him across
the breakfast table.

"No," he answered, "it's splendid—it's just like
being an Irish king." The harpist was drunker
than usual that morning when he rode away with
his harp in front of him on the pommel of his
saddle, his son trudging along behind, and when he

reached the middle of the river he fell off his horse and was nearly drowned. Later I saw what was once a harp hanging in midstream to a rock. A shattered harp clinging to a cruel rock surrounded by rushing water! I'm sure it was beautifully symbolical of something—but what?

The harpist and the mother of the boy who assists him at dances were really married, he told me, but they haven't lived together for years. Since then the boy has had a succession of informal stepmothers who never stayed very long, and just recently the harpist has really married again. In fact, the harpist's home life is typical of the matrimonial situation here, which for many reasons is endlessly interesting. Among the lower classes in Mexico " free love " is not the sociological experiment it sometimes tries to be in more civilized communities. It is a convention, an institution, and, in the existing condition of affairs, a necessity. Let me explain.

The Mexicans are an excessively passionate people and their passions develop at an early age (I employ the words in a specific sense), not only because nature has so ordered it, but because, owing to the way in which they live—whole families, not to mention animals, in a small, one-roomed house—

the elemental facts of life are known to them from the time they can see with their eyes and hear with their ears. For a Mexican child of seven or eight among the lower classes, there are no mysteries. Boys of fifteen have had their affairs with older women; boys of seventeen are usually strongly attracted by some one person whom they would like to marry. And just at this interesting and important crisis the Church furnishes the spectator with one of its disappointing and somewhat gross exhibitions.

It seems to have been proven that for people in general certain rigid social laws are a comfort and an aid to a higher, steadier standard of thought and life. In communities where such usages obtain, the ordinary person, in taking unto himself a wife, does so with a feeling of finality. On one's wedding day, but little thought is given, I fancy, to the legal loopholes of escape. It strikes one as strange, as wicked even, that a powerful Church (a Church, moreover, that regards marriage as a sacrament) should deliberately place insuperable obstacles in the path of persons who for the time being, at least, have every desire to tread the straight and narrow way. This, to its shame, the Church in Mexico does.

The only legally valid marriage ceremony in Mexico is the civil ceremony, but to a Mexican peon the civil ceremony means nothing whatever; he can't grasp its significance, and there is nothing in the prosaic, businesslike proceeding to touch his heart and stir his imagination. The only ceremony he recognizes is one conducted by a priest in a church. When he is married by a priest he believes himself to be married—which for moral and spiritual purposes is just as valuable as if he actually were. One would suppose that the Church would recognize this and encourage unions of more or less stability by making marriage inexpensive and easy. If it had the slightest desire to elevate the lower classes in Mexico from their frankly bestial attitude toward the marital relation—to inculcate ideas different and finer than those maintained by their chickens and their pigs—it could long since easily have done so. But quite simply it has no such desire. In the morality of the masses it shows no interest. For performing the marriage ceremony it charges much more than poor people can pay without going into debt. Now and then they go into debt; more often they dispense with the ceremony. On my ranch, for instance, very few of the " married " people are married. Almost every grown man lives with a woman who makes his tortillas and bears him children, and about some of these households there is an air of permanence and content. But with the death of mutual desire there is nothing that tends to turn the scale in favor of permanence; no sense of obligation, no respect for a vague authority higher and better than oneself, no adverse public opinion. Half an hour of ennui, or some one seen for a moment from a new point of view—and all is over. The man goes his way, the woman hers. The children, retaining their father's name, remain, as a rule, with the mother. And soon there is a new set of combinations. One woman who worked here had three small children—everyone with a different surname; the name of its father. While here, she kept house with the mayordomo, who for no reason in particular had wearied of the wife he had married in church. No one thought it odd that she should have three children by different men, or that she should live with the mayordomo, or that the mayordomo should tire of his wife and live with her. As a matter of fact there was nothing odd about it. No one was doing wrong, no one was "flying in the face of public opinion." She and the three men who had successively deserted her, the mayordomo who found it convenient to form

an alliance with her, and his wife, who betook herself to a neighboring ranch and annexed a boy of
sixteen, were all simply living their lives in ac-
cordance with the promptings they had never been
taught to resist. It is not unusual to hear a mother,
in a moment of irritation, exclaim, as she gives her
child a slap, " Hijo de quien sabe quien! " (Child
of who knows whom!) At an early age when they
first fall in love they would, I think, almost always prefer to be married. But where get the ten
pesos, without which the Church refuses to make
them man and wife? The idea of saving and waiting is to them, of course, utterly preposterous?
Why should it not be? What tangible advantage to them would there be in postponement?
The Church, which has always been successful in
developing and maintaining prejudices, could have
developed, had it wished to, the strongest prejudice
in favor of matrimony, and the permanence of the
marriage tie. But it has not done so, and now,
even when peons do have the religious ceremony
performed, they do not consider it binding. After
having gone to so much expense, they are not likely
to separate so soon; but that is all. One of the
men here has been married three or four times and
on every occasion he has treated himself to a re-

ligious ceremony with quite a splendid dance afterwards. As he is a skilled mason who commands
good wages and has no bad habits (except that of
getting married every little while), he can afford
it. He is a genial sort of a creature and I think
he enjoys having weddings very much as some persons enjoy having dinner parties. Sometimes he
deserts his wives and sometimes they desert him.
Of course I don't know, but I have an idea that
to have been married to him at one time or another
carries with it considerable prestige. And yet you
ask me if I am not now and then homesick for
New York!

Or did you merely ask me if I didn't find this
kind of a life desperately lonely? Everybody at
home has asked me this until I have come to believe that the modern American's greatest dread,
greater even than the dread of sickness or of death,
is the dread of being alone. But although I no
longer have it, I am able to understand it. For I
can vividly remember the time when there were
scarcely any circumstances I could not control sufficiently to insure me constant companionship. It
was novel and pleasant occasionally to putter alone
for a few hours in one's room, or in solitude to
lose oneself in an absorbing book, with the half-

formed purpose of soon finding somebody with
whom to discuss it. But to walk alone, to dine
alone, to go to the theater alone—to think alone!
To be, in a word, for any length of time, on one's
own hands—face to face with nothing but oneself! I could not possibly describe the restlessness,
the sense of " missing something," the acute melancholy I have experienced on the rare occasions when
in those days the improbable happened and for an
afternoon and evening I was left—alone. Just when
and how the change came I have no idea. Without at the moment feeling them, one acquires per-
sistent little lines that extend from the outer cor-
ners of one's eyes and almost meet the gray hairs
below and behind one's temples. The capacity—
the talent—for being alone comes to some in the
same way. With me it has been as gradual as the
accentuation of the streaks across my forehead, or
the somewhat premature blanching of the hair
around my ears. I only know that it has come
and that I am glad of it. I can be—and I sometimes am—alone indefinitely for weeks—for months
—without feeling that life is passing me by. I
may not, on the one hand, have periods of great
gayety, but on the other there is a placid kind of
satisfaction, more or less continuous, in realizing

that one's resources are a greater comfort than one's limitations are a distress. At first I was rather vain, I confess, of the facility with which I could "do without"; I used to find myself picturing certain old friends in these surroundings and despising their very probable anguish. One, I felt sure, would find his solace by perpetually dwelling in imagination upon his little triumphs of the past (there are so many kinds of little past triumphs)— in seeking to span the unspanable gulfs behind him with innumerable epistolary bridges. The eyes of another would be fixed on the far horizon; he would live through the interminable days, as so many persons live through their lives, hovering upon the brink of a vague, wonderful something that doesn't happen. Another would take to aguardiente, which is worse, they say, than morphine, and thenceforward his career would consist of trying to break himself of the habit.

But I hope I have got over being vain—indeed, I've got over being a lot of things. Solitude is a great chastener when once you accept it. It quietly eliminates all sorts of traits that were a part of you—among others, the desire to pose, to keep your best foot forever in evidence, to impress people as being something you would like to have them think you are even when you aren't. Some men I know are able to pose in solitude; had they valets they no doubt would be heroes to them. But I find it the hardest kind of work myself, and as I am lazy I have stopped trying. To act without an audience is so tiresome and unprofitable that you gradually give it up and at last forget how to act at all. For you become more interested in making the acquaintance of yourself as you really are; which is a meeting that, in the haunts of men, rarely takes place. It is gratifying, for example, to discover that you prefer to be clean rather than dirty even when there is no one but God to care which you are; just as it is amusing to note, however, that for scrupulous cleanliness you are not inclined to make superhuman sacrifices, although you used to believe you were. Clothes you learn, with something of a shock, have for you no interest whatever. You come to believe that all your life you have spent money in unnecessary raiment to please yourself only in so far as it is pleasant to gain the approval of others. You learn to regard dress merely as a covering, a precaution. For its color and its cut you care nothing.

But the greatest gift in the power of loneliness to bestow is the realization that life does not consist either of wallowing in the past or of peering anxiously at the future; and it is appalling to contemplate the great number of often painful steps by which one arrives at a truth so old, so obvious, and so frequently expressed. It is good for one to appreciate that life is now. Whether it offers little or much, life is now—this day—this hour—and is probably the only experience of the kind one is to have. As the doctor said to the woman who complained that she did not like the night air: "Madam, during certain hours of every twenty-four, night air is the only air there is." Solitude performs the inestimable service of letting us discover that it is our lives we are at every moment passing through, and not some useless, ugly, interpolated interval between what has been and what is to come. Life does not know such intervals. They can have no separate identity for they are life itself, and to realize this makes what has seemed long and without value, both precious and fleeting. The fleeting present may not be just what we once dreamed it might be, but it has the advantage of being present, whereas our past is dead and our future may never be born.

So you see, I am not lonely—or I mean, when I *am* lonely (for everyone is lonely), I try to re-

gard it as a purely objective affliction, like the sting
of a wasp, or the hot blister that comes when you
carelessly touch a leaf of mala mujer. For minor
objective afflictions there is always some sort of an
alleviator, and for loneliness I have found a remedy
in reflecting that the sensation itself is never as
interesting or as important as the circumstances that
cause it. All of which brings me back again to
this hillside clearing in the jungle with its lovely
views, its outrageous climate, its mysterious people,
its insidious fascination. Do you ever have a feeling of skepticism as to the continued existence of
places you are no longer in? I can shut my eyes
and see Boston and New York and Paris, for instance, as they are in their characteristic ways at
almost any hour of the day or night. I know just
how the people in certain quarters are conducting
themselves, where they are going next, and what
they will say and do when they arrive. But I don't
altogether believe in it. It doesn't seem possible,
somehow, that they are going ceaselessly on and on
when I am not there to see. Something happens
to places where I no longer am. Until I go back
to them I'm sure they must be white and blank like
the screen in a cinematograph performance between
the end of one film and the beginning of the next.

Just at present, nowhere is particularly existent but here.

It is a cloudless, burning day, the best kind of a day for coffee, and the asoleadero is covered with it. Through the house there is a slight stir of air, and the fact that the house-boy has just swept the floor with wet tea leaves left over from several breakfasts, makes the breeze for the moment seem cool—which it isn't. On such a day one is grateful for the bareness of a room—the smooth, unadorned walls, the hard, cool chairs. From the asoleadero comes without ceasing the harsh, hollow sound of the wooden hoes as they turn the coffee over in the sun and scrape against the cement. It is a hot and drowsy sound; the Mexican equivalent of the sound made by a lawn mower in an American " front yard " in August. It would send me to sleep, I think, if it were not counteracted by the peculiar rustling of a clump of banana trees outside the window. The slightest breath of air puts their torn ribbons into motion that is a prolonged patter, indistinguishable usually from the patter of rain. To-day it is more like the plashing of a fountain—a fountain that, on account of the goldfish, plashes gently. Whenever we need rain—and in the middle of the night I wake up and seem to hear it—it turns out to be the banana trees; but when "too much water has fallen," as they say here, and I persuade myself that this time it is only a fluttering in the banana trees, it is always rain. The whole landscape is suspended in heat haze ("swooning" is the word I should like to use, but I shan't), from the bamboo trees nodding against the sky on the crest of the hill behind the house, through the café tal in front of it, down, down the long valley between extinct, woolly looking volcanoes—thirty miles away to the sea. The sea, for some reason, never looks from this distance like the sea; it is not flat but perpendicular. I should have thought it a pale-blue wall across the valley's lower end. In an untiled corner of the piazza some chickens are taking dust baths and talking scandal in low tones; the burro, near by, has curled up in the shade like a dog and gone to sleep. I used to think I should never allow chickens to take dust baths, or burros to doze on my piazza. It seemed dreadfully squalid to permit it. Yet I have long since come to it. What can one do? Es el costumbre del pais. So, also, is the custom of letting a few fastidious hens lay eggs in one's bed. But I have always been very firm about that.

Except for the chickens and the burro, the two men on the asoleadero, a buzzard resting on the limb of a dead tree, and one of the dogs who has sneaked into the house to get rid of the flies, and who thinks that because I didn't turn him out I didn't see him, there is apparently nothing alive in the whole world. And their animation is but a tranquil stupor. It does not seem as if anything could ever happen here to disturb one. I'm sure I look as if I had been dreaming forever, but so far to-day (it is only half past two) there have been the following demands upon my time and attention:

At seven, one of the men tapped on my window and said he was going to town, so I got up, wrote a note for him to post, made out the list for the grocer—sugar, onions, flour, bread, a new bottle of olive oil, two brooms, and a mouse trap—and gave him a hundred-peso bill to change somewhere in the village into silver, as to-morrow is pay day. It is inconvenient, but in the country one has to pay wages—even enormous sums like five and ten pesos—in silver. Indians don't understand paper money as a rule and won't take it; the others, too, are sometimes suspicious of it—which is a survival, I suppose, of the time when several different governments were trying to run Mexico at once and the bank notes of one state were not accepted in another. At least that is the only way I can account for their reluctance to be paid in good paper money. A man I know got tired of sending every week to town for bags of silver, and told the people on his place that a law had been passed (Oh, those laws!) permitting an employer to pay only half as much as he owed to persons who refused bills. Thereafter bills were not scorned. No doubt I could say something of the same kind, but more than enough laws of this sort are " passed " in darkest Mexico as it is. I shouldn't care to be responsible for another. In the kitchen there were no evidences of activity on the part of Rosalía, and as I was beginning to be hungry I knocked on her door and asked her (although I knew only too well) what was the matter. She moaned back that she was very sick and believed she was going to die. I didn't tell her I hoped she would, although the thought occurred to me. For the trouble with Doña Rosalía was that she went to a dance last night at a little ranch next to mine, stayed until half past four, and was carried home stinko. This I had gleaned from Ramón (he who went to town), who had helped to carry her. With the ladies at

the party she had consumed many glasses of a comparatively harmless although repulsive mixture of
eggs, sugar, milk, and brandy, prettily named ron-
poco. With the gentlemen, however, she had
laughingly tossed off eight or ten drinks of aguardiente, not to record an occasional glass of sherry,
until at last the gentlemen were obliged laughingly
to toss her by the head and feet into a corner, where
she lay until they carried her home in the rosy dawn.
I don't know what to do about Rosalía. She is
an odious woman. If she would content herself
with one lover—somebody I know—I shouldn't
mind in the least. But she has a different one every
week—persons I've never laid eyes on usually—and
it makes me nervous to think that there are strange
men in the house at night. Recently I have resorted to locking the kitchen door at a respectable
hour and removing the key, which has made her
furious, as I have not been in the habit of locking any doors and as I did it without offering an
explanation. Her room, furthermore, is without a
window. I shouldn't be surprised if she tried to
poison me; they are great little poisoners. So I
had to stand for half an hour or more fanning a
fire built of green, damp wood, and getting my
own breakfast—an orange, a cup of tea, some eggs,

and a roll without butter. The butter habit has been eliminated along with many others. I could get good, pure American butter dyed with carrot juice and preserved in boracic or salicylic acid, by sending to the City of Mexico, but it is too much bother.

After breakfast I walked over to where they are picking. I can't, of course, help in the picking, but frequent, unexpected appearances on my part are not without value. If they were sure I weren't coming they would, in their zeal to tear off many berries quickly (they are paid by the amount they pick), break the branches and injure the trees. As they have no respect for their own property I suppose it would be fatuous to count on any respect for mine. When I got back to the house I began to write to you, but before I had covered half a page, one Lucio appeared on the piazza, apparently for the purpose of chatting interminably about the weather, the coffee, the fact that some one had died and some one else was about to be born; none of which topics had anything to do with the real object of his visit. Three quarters of an hour went by before he could bring himself to ask me to lend him money with which to buy two marvelously beautiful pigs. I was kind, but I was firm. I don't mind lending money for most needs, but I refuse to encourage hogriculture. It is too harrowing. When they keep pigs, no day goes by that the poor, obese things do not escape and, helplessly rolling and stumbling down the hill, squeal past the house with a dog attached to every ear. Besides, they root up the young coffee trees. No, Lucio, no. Chickens, ducks, turkeys, cows, lions, and tigers if you must, but not pigs. Lucio—inscrutable person that he is—perfectly agrees with me. As he says good-by one would think he had originally come not to praise pigs but to protest against them. After his departure there are at least fifteen minutes of absolute quiet.

Then arrive a party of four—two men and two women—respectable-looking, well-mannered people, who stand on the piazza saying good morning and inquiring after my health. I have never seen them before, but I stop my letter and go out to talk to them, wondering all the while where they have come from and what they want—for, of course, they want something; everybody always does. For an interminable time their object does not emerge and in the face of such pretty, pleasant manners it is out of the question for me bluntly to demand, "What have you come for?" In despair I ask

them if they would like to see the house, and as
they stand in my bare sala, commenting in awed
undertones, I have a sudden penetrating flash of
insight into the relativeness of earthly grandeur.
To me the sala is the clean, ascetic habitation of one
who has not only realized what is and what is not
essential, but who realizes that every new nail, pane
of glass, tin of paint, and cake of soap is brought
sixty or seventy miles through seas of mud and
down a precipice three or four thousand feet high
on the back of a weary mule. To them, the simple
interior is a miracle of ingenious luxury. They
gaze at the clumsy fireplace, touch it, try to see daylight through the chimney and fail to grasp its purpose, although they revere it as something superbly
unnecessary that cost untold sums. The plated
candlesticks on the table are too bewildering to
remark on at all; they will refer to them on the
way home. The kitchen range at first means nothing to anyone, but when I account for it as an
American brasero the women are enthralled. One
of them confesses she thought it was a musical instrument—the kind they have in church! There
is nothing more to exhibit, nothing more to talk
about, so during a general silence one of the men
asks me if I will sell them a little corn—enough to

keep them for two days—and I know they have come to the point at last. They work on a ranch a mile or so away and the owner, an Englishman, who lives in town, has forgotten or neglected to supply them; they have none left for their tortillas. I am not at all anxious to part with any of my corn, but I desire to be obliging both to them and the Englishman, who, of course, will be told of it the next time he rides out to his ranch. The house-boy having disappeared in search of firewood, I have to measure the corn myself; all of which takes time.

Next, a little boy to buy a pound of lard. (As a convenience I sell lard at cost.) Then a little girl to say her mother is tired and would like a drink of aguardiente. As her mother cooks for eighteen men who are working here temporarily without their families, no doubt she deserves one. Anyhow she gets it. Rosalía and the house-boy usually dole out corn, lard, and aguardiente, but Rosalía is still in a trance and the boy has not returned. Then Ezequiel, father of Candelario, stops on his way over to the coffee tanks to tell me that Candelario is sick and he would like me to prescribe. As Candelario is one of my godchildren I have to show more interest in him than I feel.

"He's always sick, Ezequiel," I answer; "my medicines don't seem to do him good!" Ezequiel agrees with me that they don't. "Except for his stomach, which is swollen, he has been getting thinner and weaker for a long time. Have you any idea of the cause?" Ezequiel, staring fixedly at his toes, confesses that he has.

"What is it?"

"I am ashamed to tell you."

"Don't be ashamed; I shan't speak of it, and if I know the cause I may be able to do some good." Ezequiel, still intent upon his toes, suddenly looks up and blurts out:

"He's a dirt eater."

"Oh, well—that accounts for it. Why don't you make him stop?" I ask, at which Candelario's father shrugs hopelessly.

And well he may, for dirt eating seems to be a habit or a vice or a disease, impossible to cure. Many of them have it—grown persons as well as children—and in the interest of science, or morbid curiosity, perhaps, I have tried, but with little success, to get some definite information on the subject. Nobody here who drinks to excess objects to admitting he is a drunkard. He will refer to himself rather proudly as "hombre perdido" (a lost man), and expect to be patted on the back. But I have known a dirt eater to deny he was one even after a surgeon, to save his life, had operated on him and removed large quantities of dirt. As the habit is considered a shameful one, information at first hand is impossible to acquire. Candelario, for instance, is only seven, but although his father and mother know he is a dirt eater, they have never caught him in the act. "We have watched him all day sometimes," Ezequiel declared, "every minute; and he would lie awake at night until we were both asleep and then crawl out of the house to get it." Whether there is a particular kind of soil to which the victims are addicted or whether any sufficiently gritty substance will do, I don't know; neither does Ezequiel. Among foreigners here the theory is that their stomachs have become apathetic to the assaults of chile and demand an even more brutal form of irritation. General emaciation and an abdominal toy balloon are the outward and visible signs of the habit which can be broken they say only by death. One woman on the place died of it last year, and her seventeen-year-old son, who must have begun at an early age as his physical development is that of a sickly child of ten, is not long for this world. There was nothing I

could do for my unfortunate little godchild, and
Ezequiel walked slowly away, looking as depressed
as I felt. For Candelario is a handsome, intelligent little boy and deserves a better fate. But—
"esterá mejor con Dios!" (He'll be better off
with God.)

From then until luncheon there is comparative
peace. That is to say, when I am disturbed I am
not disturbed for long at a time. A breathless
woman comes to "get something" for her husband
who has just been bitten in the foot by a snake.
As she is scared, she omits the customary preludes
and I get rid of her within ten minutes. I have
a hypodermic injection for snake bites that comes
from Belgium in little sealed bottles and seems to be
efficacious, but as the snake that bit her husband was
very small (a bravo amarillo, I think she named
it), and as he had been bitten, unsuccessfully, four
years ago by another member of the same family,
I do not waste one on him. Instead, I send him
several drinks of ammonia and water which may
or may not have any effect on snake bites. To tell
the truth, I don't care. The house-boy on returning from the mountain with a mule-load of
firewood declares that the occasion is auspicious for
anointing one of the dogs who has the mange. As

the application of the salve is painful to the dog who endeavors to bite the boy, it is necessary for me to pat the poor thing's head and engage him in conversation while the boy craftily dabs and smears in the rear. When this precarious performance is taking place I notice a turkey, a magnificent and sedate bird, who seems completely to have lost his ordinarily fine mind. He is rushing about in a most agonized fashion, beating his head in the dust, at times pausing and—perhaps I imagine it—turning pale and looking as if he were about to faint.

"Manuel—what on earth is the matter with him? He has gone crazy," I exclaim.

"Oh, no," Manuel placidly answers, "he fought so much with the other turkeys and with some of the roosters as well, that I stuck a feather through his nostrils. I thought it might *divert his attention*." And he smilingly waits for me to praise his thoughtful ingenuity.

It takes us fifteen minutes to catch the distracted turkey and remove the feather. By that time I am, in every sense, too overheated to permit myself to talk to Manuel on the subject of cruelty to animals. Some time when I have just had a bath, put on a fresh suit of white clothes, and am feeling altogether cool and calm and kind, I shall tell him a few things. But to what end? If he had been willfully, deliberately cruel to the turkey there might be some hope of converting him—of bringing about a change of heart. But he wasn't consciously cruel. Like most Mexicans he is fond of animals. In fact, there is in Mexico more emotion expended on pet animals than in any country I know. They make pets of their sheep and their pigs, and one frequently sees a child sitting in a doorway or by the roadside nursing a contented chicken. Yet in emotion it more often than not begins and ends. Their lack of real kindness, of consideration, of thought, in a word, is infuriating. Everyone on the ranch has dogs, and at times they are petted, played with, admired, and called by affectionate names— but they are never fed. I have seen a family go into ecstasies for hours at a time over six new-born puppies and then merely shrug and change the subject when it was suggested that they ought to feed the pitifully thin little mother. The national love of grace and beauty renders them sensitive to the beauty and grace of animals, but to their comforts, even their necessities, they are blind and therefore indifferent. They are all rather incapable of divided feelings. Manuel had not the slightest feeling of compassion for the turkey's torture.

The fact that he had prevented the bird from fighting was all sufficient and left no room in his intelligence for any other.

Rosalía heroically manages to cook and serve my luncheon, and as she drags herself in and out, the color of a faded lettuce leaf, with her rebozo over one eye, I almost feel sorry for her. But I steel my heart and make no comment either on her illness or her partial recovery. After luncheon I again take my intermittent pen in hand and immediately throw it down. There is a scurrying of bare feet on the piazza and six of the carpenter's sons gather about the door. They are all crying and, although it is no doubt physiologically impossible, they are all about ten years old. The carpenter has eight sons, but one is noticeably younger and the other is an infant in arms.

"What has happened?" I ask serenely; for I have grown to regard battle, murder, and sudden death as conventional forms of relaxation. Six, sobbing, simultaneous versions of the tragedy leave me ignorant.

"Now, one of you come in—you, Florenzio— and tell me about it. All the others go around to the kitchen and tell Doña Rosalía. Now then, Florenzio, be a man and stop crying. What is it?"

I demand. Florenzio's narrative has moments of coherence. His father (usually the best of fathers) went to the dance last night and came home drunk (he rarely drinks). This morning, as he felt so badly, he tried to " cure " himself (they always do) by drinking a little more. By ten o'clock he was all right, and then—and then, "*he passed the cure!*" (This, I think, is one of the most delightful phrases in the language.) After he had " passed the cure " he suddenly went crazy, smashed all the cooking utensils on the floor, and ended by seizing a stick of wood from the brasero and beating his wife to a pulp. Then tearing the baby from her breast he reeled with it into the jungle.

"All of which, my dear Florenzio," I feel like saying, " is dramatic and fascinating—but where do *I* come in? I can't undertake to pursue your estimable father into the jungle, and I have no desire to inspect the maternal pulp. Why have you come to *me*?" But, of course, I say nothing of the kind. Instead, I am sympathetic and aghast and, surrounded by six fluttering little carpenters, go over to their hut, exclaim at the broken pottery, condole with the pulp, moan about the evils of drink, declare that everything will come out satisfactorily in the end, and leave them tear-blotted but not without interest in the future.

What, however, was in my thoughts throughout the visit was not the immediate distress of this particular family, but the long distress which, it sometimes seems to me, is the life of all of them. The house was typical of the houses on my place—of the houses everywhere in this part of the country, and I groaned that it should be. A small inclosure of bamboo, fourteen feet by twelve perhaps, the steep, pointed roof covered with rough, hand-made shingles of a soft wood that soon rots and leaks. The bamboo, being no more than a lattice, affords but slight protection from a slanting rain and none whatever from the wind; the dirt floor, therefore, is damp everywhere, and near the walls muddy. At one end is a brasero—not the neat, tiled affair for charcoal, with holes on top and draughts in the side that one sees in towns, but a kind of box made of logs, raised from the ground on rough legs and filled with hard earth. A small fire of green wood smolders in the center of this, filling the room from time to time with blinding smoke, and around it (before the carpenter passed his cure) were three or four jars of coarse brown pottery, and a thin round platter of unglazed earthenware on which

are baked the tortillas. Near by is a black stone
with a slight concavity on its upper surface and a
primitive rolling pin of the same substance resting
upon it. On the floor in the corner are some frayed
petates—thin mats woven of palm or rushes. This
is all, and this is home. At night the family hud-
dles together for warmth with nothing but the
petates between them and the damp ground. They
sleep in their clothes and try to cover themselves
with their well-worn sarapes.

In a perpetually warm climate there is nothing
deplorable about such habitations, but from Novem-
ber to March the tierra templada is not perpetually
warm; it is for weeks at a time searchingly cold.
The thermometer often goes down to forty (Fahren-
heit), and forty with a mad, wet wind blowing
through the house is agony to a person in cotton
pajamas, trying to seek repose in a mud puddle.
During a protracted norther the sadness of their
faces, the languor of their movements—the silent,
patient wretchedness of them is indescribably depressing. A week or so ago during a norther, when
I was taking a walk between the end of one cloud
burst and the beginning of the next, I stopped
to pay my respects to a baby who had been born
a few days before. The mother was vigorously

kneading corn with her stone rolling pin and the baby, absolutely naked on a blanket, was having a chill.

"The poor little thing is very cold; it is shaking all over," I remarked.

"Yes, it has had chills ever since it came," the woman answered.

"But in weather like this you ought to cover it," I insisted.

"It doesn't seem to wish to be covered," was the reply. Upon which I observed that it was a very pretty baby, and departed in tears. When one lives among them one marvels, not like the tourist of a week, that they are dirty, but that under the circumstances they are as clean as they are; not that so many of them are continually sick, but that any of them are ever well; not that they love to get drunk, but that they can bear to remain sober.

And yet, even in cold, wet weather I am sure some of my pity is wasted. If that baby lives and grows to manhood, a damp petate on the ground and a thin blanket will be the only bed in its recollection; a hut of openwork bamboo (or, at the most elaborate, of rough boards an inch apart) its only shelter from the rain and wind. Furthermore, a human being is never suffering as acutely as one sometimes thinks he is, if he fails to take advantage of every available means of alleviating his condition. Often when the faces of these people are wan with cold, I have asked them why they do not stuff the cracks in their houses and keep out the wind. The jungle a hundred yards away is all the year luxuriant with great waterproof leaves, which when hung on walls or piled on roofs are as impermeable as if they were patented and cost money. No one is ignorant of their use, for the north side of almost every house (it is from the north that the cold winds blow here) is adorned with them. But why only the north side? If I knew beforehand that I should have to spend a week in one of these huts I should, with a machete and two or three hours of effort, make it warm and habitable. But they, knowing that they will live and die in one, barely protect the north side, sheath their machetes, cover their noses with their sarapes, and shiver in silence. To the question, "Why don't you make your house warm and dry with leaves?" I have never been given a definite or satisfactory answer. So sketchy and evasive have been the replies that I am actually unable to remember what any of them were. In fact, Mexicans have a genius for stringing words upon a flashing chain of shrugs and smiles—of presenting you with a verbal rosary which later you find yourself unable to tell.

Such, so far, has been my day. The general outline of the rest of it I could draw with closed eyes. In another hour the sun will have begun to lose its drying powers and I shall go over to the asoleadero to watch the men pack the half-dried coffee into bags and pile them up under cover for the night. By that time the pickers will have begun to straggle back through the trees—the women and children talking in tired, quiet voices, the men silent and bent double under their loads of berries. Where we are—with a hill between us and the western sky—dusk will overtake us while the mountains opposite and the distant gulf are still tinted with sunset lights of unimagined delicacy; we shall have to measure the berries and record the amounts picked by the flame of a torch. Then everyone will mysteriously fade away among the trees, and before going back to the house I shall linger alone a moment to look at the black tracery of the bamboo plumes against the yellow afterglow, with a single star trembling through an azure lake above them —perhaps I shall wait for the moon to come out of the gulf and disperse the silver moon mist that already has begun to gather on the horizon. The world will seem to be a very quiet one—not silent with the intense and terrifying silence of desert places, but peacefully, domestically silent. For through the brief twilight will drift detached and softened notes of life—the pat, pat, patting of a tortilla, the disembodied rhythm of a guitar, the baying of a hound.

At dinner Rosalía will have sufficiently recovered to relate to me, as she comes and goes from the kitchen, all she can remember about the dance of the night before—new scandals to gloat over, new elopements to prophesy. What she can't remember she will gliby invent. The mayordomo will come in to report on the coffee, the house-boy will tell me who has bought corn and lard, and in what amounts. (He can't write but he has the memory of a phonograph.) If the novel you sent me—it came yesterday—is as good as you say it is, I shall forget for the next few hours that Mexico was ever discovered. I used to wonder in bookstores how anyone could have the effrontery to print another book, but now, since they have entirely taken the place that used to be filled for me by more or less intelligent conversation, I feel like composing a letter of thanks for every new writer I hear of.

Before going to bed I shall walk around the piazza to see that none of the men who have been chatting in the moonlight have set the place on fire with their cigarettes. One night I stooped down to pick up my little black dog who sleeps there, exclaiming as I clutched him, "Kitsy, kitsy, kitsy —who's uncle's darling!" or some equally dignified remark. But it wasn't the little black dog at all —it was the head of an Indian who was spending the night there, covered, except for his shock of hair, with empty coffee sacks. To-morrow will be just like to-day.

But perhaps I should not say exactly that, for I recall the reply of the German clerk who was asked if he did not find his occupation monotonous. "Why, no," he said. "To-day, for instance, I am dating everything June 3d. To-morrow, I shall write June 4th, and the day after, June 5th. You see—in my work there is constant variety." And so it is here. To-morrow, no doubt, it will be wet and cool instead of dry and hot; the dispulpador may refuse to work (it is almost time for it to get out of order again), and I have a feeling that the bamboo trough, in which the water runs a quarter of a mile from its source to the washing tanks, is about due to collapse somewhere. Then, some one will have a quarrel with his wife and come to tell me that they are going to leave. This is a most inexplicable phase of them. When they have a quarrel their one idea, apparently, is to pack up their few possessions and seek a change of scene. If it were to get rid of each other I could understand it; but they often depart together! After dark a clacuache (I don't know how to spell him, but that is the way he is pronounced) may sneak upon the chickens and succeed in getting one of them. Not long ago a wild boar—we have them here; small but fierce—trotted out of the jungle and attacked a young girl who was sewing in front of her family residence. She happened to be alone and the little brute would have killed her if some dogs had not come to her rescue. Perhaps it will happen again. A few nights ago while I was reading in the sala, I heard a light clatter of hoofs on the tiles of the piazza. When I turned from the lamp to look out, a deer stood peering in at me through the open door. For a quarter of a minute I almost believed he would end by coming in and putting his head on my lap; I sat so motionless and tried so hard to will him to. But he reared back and the door-way was once more a frame without a picture. The next afternoon some one on the place shot a deer

and tried to sell me a piece of it, but, although I
hadn't had meat for days, I couldn't bring myself
to buy any. Then, too, it is about time for somebody—somebody very young or very old—to die.
Death here is more than death; it is a social opportunity. I always go to the wakes, both because
I know my presence adds interest and éclat to the
occasions and because I enjoy them. Everybody
(except me) sits on the floor—the women draped
in their rebozos as if they were in church—while the
deceased, in a corner of the room, with candles at
its head and feet, and wild flowers on the wall
above it, seems somehow to take a pallid interest
in what goes on. I do not sit on the floor because
the bereaved family has borrowed a chair from
Rosalía in the hope that I would come. But when
I take possession of it I, of course, do not let on
that I know it belongs to me. For an hour, perhaps, while other guests silently emerge from the
jungle and sidle quietly into the room, the conversation is in undertones and fragmentary. The dead
is referred to with affection or respect; the most
conventional conventions are, in a word, observed.
Later, however, refreshments are handed about by
the surviving members of the household; the ladies
partake of sherry, the gentlemen outside relieve the

tension with aguardiente. Gradually the atmosphere of the gathering becomes less formal; talk is more sustained and resumes the flexibility of every day. Trinidad indulges in a prolonged reminiscence which Rosalía caps with a brilliant and slightly indecent anecdote that makes everyone laugh. Outside the men have another drink of aguardiente, and seating themselves on the ground begin to play cards by the light of a torch. Suddenly there is a dog fight. In some way the writhing, shrieking, frantic, hairy bodies roll past the card players and into the room among the women and children. Everyone screams, and from my chair (I am now not sitting, but standing on it) the floor is an indescribable chaos. After this it is impossible to reconstruct a house of sorrow. The deceased is not exactly forgotten, but it no longer usurps the center of the stage. No one can quite resume the mood in which he came, and from then on the wake is in every respect like a dance except for the facts that there is a dead person in the room and that there is no dancing. In the small hours, some thrifty guest opens a cantina and does a good business in aguardiente and sherry, in tortillas, tamales, bread, and coffee. I do not often stay so late.

Now and then I have to go to the village and

be godfather for some infant born on the place, and occasionally the festivities that follow a wedding—the dancing and drinking, card playing and fighting—vary the monotony of my long, quiet evenings. Last year a man I know, who has a cattle ranch a day and a half away from here, issued a general invitation to the countryside to come to his place and be married free of charge. He built a temporary chapel and hired a priest and for two days the hymeneal torch flamed as it never had in that part of the world before. So many persons took advantage of the opportunity that the priest, who began by marrying a couple at a time, was obliged toward the last to line them up in little squads of six and eight and ten and let them have it, so to speak, by the wholesale. It was pathetic to see old men and women with their children and their children's children all waiting in the same group to be married.

Once in a long, long while I have a visitor—a real visitor I mean; some one who stays a week or two, sits opposite me at meals and, to all intents and purposes, talks my own language. You can scarcely —in fact, you cannot at all—imagine just what this means, or the light in which I view it. It is a different light; " a light that never was " in localities where, in the matter of companionship for an evening, there is an embarrassment of choice—where one becomes a kind of selfish, social epicure. You know how you go into your club sometimes at half past six or seven, wondering vaguely with whom you will dine. There are fifteen or twenty more or less civilized young men sitting about drinking cocktails, over whom, as you pretend to be reading the headlines of the evening paper, you cast an appraising eye. Most of them are going to dine at the club and almost any one of them would suggest your joining his group if you gave him the necessary chance. But, unwilling to commit yourself, you let the time slip by and, unless you see somebody in whom you are especially interested, you end by dining with the newspaper. Or if you do bind yourself to any particular party and table and hour, you often find yourself regretting the act even while you commit it. You haven't, after all, really anything in common with the persons in whose company you are destined to spend the next hour and a half, you reflect, and a thousand such dinners would bring you no nearer to them.

But in a place like this how different it is! It is the difference between looking at things through a telescope and through a microscope. At home we have opportunity and time only to make use of the larger, sketchier instrument; after we pass a certain age we rarely learn to know anyone with the searching intimacy that was the point and joy and sorrow of our earlier friendships. Here, however, not from inclination but from force of circumstances, there is now and then a pale afterglow of the old relations. A visitor here is necessarily an isolated specimen, and as such he is obliged for the time being to regard me. For a week or so we see each other at rather terribly close range and the experience is valuable. For it sends home to roost still another platitude, and it is only by accepting and realizing the truth of platitudes that we grow wise and tolerant and kinder. It used to bore me beyond the power of expression to read or to be told that " everybody has good qualities and an interesting side, if you only know how to get at them," and I still would enjoy kicking the person who informs me of this fact with the air of one who lives on the heights, yet who is not above showing the way to others groping in the valley. But although I have not yet arrived at the point where I like to acknowledge it, I have learned to believe that it is true. Perhaps it was to this end that I was sent here. Quien sabe?

VIII

WEALTH, education, and travel often combine to render unimportant, persons who, had they stayed at home in a state of comparative poverty and ignorance, would, perhaps, have been worthy of one's serious consideration. For money, books, and the habit of " going a journey " tend to draw their possessors toward the symmetrical eddy known as " society," and society cannot for long endure anything essentially unlike itself. One's lot may be cast in New York, Paris, London, St. Petersburg, Rome, Madrid, or the City of Mexico, but in so far as one is " in society " in any of those places one conforms, outwardly at least, to a system of ethics, etiquette, dress, food, drink, and division of time that obtains, with a few local differences, in all the others. My acquaintance among Mexicans of wealth, education, and extensive experience is not, I confess, numerous, but it is sufficient constantly to remind me of that ever-increasing " smallness of the world " we hear so much about, and to impress upon me how distress-

ingly nice and similar are persons the world over
who have money, education, the habit of society, and
little else. One Mexican family I happened not
long ago to see every day for three months was
an excellent example of this pleasant, cosmopolitan
blight. They somehow ought to have been as florid
and real, as indigenous to the volcanic soil, as were
the hundred and fifty others (we were at a small
" health resort ") who had gathered under the same
roof from all parts of the republic. Papa *ought*
to have joined in the noisy, frantic games in the
sala after dinner and with a complete and engaging lack of self-consciousness made a monkey of
himself, as did the other men; mamma *ought* to
have come to breakfast in an unbelted dressing sack
with her long, black, wet hair hanging down her
back against a blue or yellow bath towel attached
by safety pins to her shoulders, as did her lady compatriots. The little daughter *ought* to have worn
beruffled dresses of some inexpensive but gaudy
fabric (scarlet gingham trimmed with coarse lace,
for instance), and on Sunday a pair of rather soiled,
high-buttoned shoes of white or pale-blue kid. The
son—a youth of twenty-two—*ought* to have been
an infinitely more tropical young man than he was;
more emphatic and gesticulative in conversation,

more obviously satisfied with. himself, and as to his clothes, just a trifle wrong in every important detail.

But papa, who was a lawyer of some note, had been in the diplomatic service, and although one evening he did gravely take part in a game of "Button! button! Who's got the button?" he never permitted himself the graceful and popular diversion of dredging with his teeth for ten-cent pieces in a bowl of flour. Mamma not only did not squalidly appear at breakfast with her hair down—she did not appear at breakfast at all. The little girl dressed sometimes in the English fashion, sometimes in the French, and at all times was able to chatter fluently and idiomatically in four languages. The young man, in spite of his American and English clothes, could not have been mistaken for an American or an Englishman, but he might have been, at first sight, almost anything else. They had lived abroad—in France, in Belgium, in Germany—and they had lost their tags. They very much resembled the sort of persons one is invited to meet at dinner almost anywhere; persons who wear the right clothes, use the right fork, who neither come too early nor stay too late and to whom it is second nature to talk for three hours about nothing at all, with ease, amiability, and an appearance of interest.

Their house in the City of Mexico was like themselves. It had, so to speak, been born Mexican and then denationalized. For although it had been built with a patio and tiled floors on the assumption that the climate of Mexico is hot, it had acquired half a dozen fireplaces, a complete epidermis of Oriental rugs, pretty and comfortable furniture, pictures that did not merely make one giggle, bric-a-brac that did not merely make one sick, a distinct personality, an atmosphere of comfort and all the other attributes a genuinely Mexican interior invariably lacks. It would be amusing to blindfold somebody in New York or London, transport him on a magic carpet to one of the señora's dinner parties or afternoons at home, and ask him to guess where he was.

However much at a loss he might be for an answer in this particular instance, it would be impossible for him, on the other hand, to mistake his whereabouts could he be suddenly wafted to the little coffee town of Rebozo and set down in the abode of my friend, Don Juan Valera. For although it is said that Don Juan's estimable wife has the tidy sum of a million dollars coming to her on the death of her father, and Don Juan has proved himself as discreet in the coffee business as he was in the business of matrimony, he is not a citizen of the world. A visit to Don Juan's is an all-day affair—exhausting, ruinous to the digestion, quite delightful, and Mexican from beginning to end. In fact, there is about provincial Mexican hospitality a quality for which I can think of no more descriptive phrase than "old-fashioned." It has a simplicity, a completeness, an amplitude that, to one who is accustomed to the quick, well-ordered festivities of modern civilization, seem to belong to a remote period, the period of "old times." We left Barranca at half past eight in the morning—enthusiastic, vivacious, amiable, and, in appearance, not, I am told, unprepossessing. We returned at seven in the evening—depleted, silent, irritable, and ages older-looking than our ages.

The train to Rebozo, where lives Don Juan, slides circuitously down the foothills through almost a tunnel of tropical vegetation and emerges at last in one of the great gardens of the world. One does not soon grow indifferent to tropical foliage. Even when one has come to the conclusion that there is after all nothing more wonderful in a gully full of plumelike ferns, twenty and thirty feet high, than in a row of familiar elm or maple trees, one involuntarily hangs out of the window to marvel at the ferns. The green, damp jungle depths, partly veiled in smoky vapor that detaches itself, sails diagonally up the hillside and then shreds into nothingness as the hot sunlight finds its way through the trees, recall "transformation scenes" at the theater, or long-forgotten pictures in old geographies. It is difficult for a Northerner simply to take their beauty for granted, as he does the beauty of trees and shrubs at home, for there is about nature in the tropics always a suggestion of mystery, suffocation—evil. I do not know if it is because one is reasonably suspicious of venomous snakes, poisonous plants, and nameless, terrifying insects, but tropical nature, however exquisite, inspires neither confidence nor affection. The poet who first apostrophized "Mother Nature" never put on a pair of poison-proof gloves and endeavored to hack a path through jungle with a machete. In the tropics, the bosom of Mother Nature does not invite her children to repose.

Don Juan met us at the train—which deposits its passengers in the middle of Rebozo's principal street—and, as it was still early in the morning and there were nine hours of sixty minutes each ahead

of us, most of which we were aware would have
to be consumed in sawing conversational wood at
Don Juan's, we called first upon the family of Don
Pedro Valasquez — another local coffee magnate.
Don Pedro's wife—in a pink cotton wrapper, with
her hair down, but heavily powdered and asphyxi-
atingly perfumed—had no doubt seen us get off the
train, for she met us at the front door, kissed the
two girls in our party (who, after calling on Mexican ladies, always declare they have contracted lead-
poisoning), and, chattering like a strange but kindly
bird, took us into the sala.

There is in all truly Mexican salas a striking—
a depressing—similarity one does not notice in the
drawing-rooms of other countries. It is as if there
were, somewhere in the republic, a sort of standard
sala—just as there is in a glass case at Washington
a standard of weight and a standard of measure-
ment—which all the other salas try, now humbly,
now magnificently, to approximate. I have sat in
many Mexican salas and I have peeped from the
street into many more, but it would be difficult if
not impossible for me to know whether I were in
the house of Don This rather than in the house
of Don That, if none of the family were present to
give me a clew. They are all long and high and

bleak. In the exact geometric center is a table with nothing on it but its chilly marble top. Over it hangs an electric chandelier (the unshaded incandescent light, like a bad deed in an excellent world, casts its little beam almost everywhere in Mexico), the size and elaborateness of which is a tolerably accurate symptom of the owner's wealth and position. Around the walls is placed at intervals, as regular as the architecture will allow, a " set " of furniture—usually of Austrian bentwood with rattan seats and backs—the kind that looks as if it were made of gas pipe painted black. Near the heavily barred windows, where they can be admired by the passers-by, are other marble-topped tables laden with trivial imported objects of china and glass and metal: bisque figurines painted in gay colors, little ornate vases that could not hold a single flower, fanciful inkstands, and statuettes of animals — rabbits and dogs and owls — standing about on mats horribly evolved out of worsted and beads. The few pictures are usually vivid in color and obvious in sentiment.

In fact, the prominence given in Mexican houses to advertisements of brewers and grocers—calendars portraying, for example, a red-cheeked young person with two horticulturally improbable cherries dangling from her faultless mouth—is indicative of the warm, bright school of art for which the nation really cares. The floor is of tiles—sometimes light-colored and ornamented, but more often dark-red and plain—and the ceiling is almost invariably a false ceiling of painted canvas that eventually sags a trifle and somewhat disturbs a stranger accustomed to ceilings of plaster by spectrally rising and falling in the breeze. In hot weather the bareness and hardness and cleanliness of these places, the absence of upholstery and yielding surfaces, the fact that the floors can be sprinkled and swabbed off with a wet mop, are most agreeable. But whereas in some parts of Mexico one or two days of a month may be warm and the other twenty-nine or thirty cool or even cold, the sala, with its inevitable echo, frozen floors, and pitiless draughts, is usually as inviting as a mortuary chapel. Don Pedro's, besides containing precisely what I have enumerated, had an upright piano, a canary, and a phonograph, and if I had needed any proof of the fact that Mexican nerves are of an entirely different quality from our own, the hour and a half we spent there would have supplied it.

In the first place, when " entertaining company " in Mexico everybody talks all the time, nobody listens, and the voices of the women are more often than not loud and harsh. When they hit upon a subject with possibilities in the way of narrative and detail, they cling to it, develop it, expand it, and exhaust it, and then go back and do it all over again. On this occasion the topic that naturally suggested itself when Don Pedro appeared, limping slightly and leaning on the arm of one of his daughters, was the accident he had met with some months before while out riding with three of the Americans who were now calling on him. There was the usual preliminary skirmish of politeness, and then followed the conversational engagement. It lasted for an hour and a quarter, and except for the fact that during its progress one of my compatriots developed a headache and I became temporarily deaf, it was no doubt a draw. Don Pedro told *his* story, which began with the pedigree and biography of the horse that had thrown him, the combination of circumstances that had led up to his riding him instead of some other horse, the nature of the weather on that historical morning, the condition of the roads, the various careless happy thoughts and remarks he had indulged in just before the fatal moment, the fatal moment itself, the sensations and reflections of a Mexican gentleman on returning to consciousness after a bump on the head——

But it must not be supposed that anyone except me (who had not been present at the accident) was listening to Don Pedro or paying the slightest attention to him. His wife, with hands outstretched and flung in the air, with eyes now rolling, now flashing, was screaming *her* version; just how she had spent her time between the departure of the blithesome cavalcade and its unexpected appearance with a litter in its midst; what she had unsuspectingly remarked to her daughter and one of the servants when first she descried it; what they had respectively replied; what she did next, and what she did after that and the sensations of a Mexican lady on hearing that her husband had been thrown from his horse and rendered unconscious——

My three American friends, who live in Mexico and have learned how to project themselves into the spirit of every social situation, were meeting the demands of the moment by bellowing *their* more or less fictitious tales, and in the narrow street beyond the long open windows, the train we had just left (it was so near we could have leaned out and touched it) was making wholly unsuccessful efforts to return to Barranca. The whistle and bell of the engine shrieked and rang incessantly, the cars separated in an agony of noise and then slam-banged together again and again and again. Most of the time the engine was in front of the house sending a geyser of hoarse steam through one of the sala windows. When the six simultaneous narratives were nearing their climaxes and the train was at its loudest, a little girl came into the room, sat down at the piano, and began to practice scales, a little boy appeared from the patio for the pur-pose of making the phonograph play the sextette from " Lucia," as rendered by four trombones and two cornets, and the canary bird went abruptly and completely mad. Most of this lasted without sur-cease for an hour and a quarter. The last fifteen minutes we spent in saying good-by. The señora kissed the two ladies before we left the sala, and again at the door. They were more than ordinarily convinced that they had contracted lead-poisoning. Then we strolled away to the house of Don Juan Valera, where we were received by Don Juan's wife and five enchanting children, his mother who had come over from a neighboring village to cook her son's birthday dinner (she was ninety-three and as bald as an egg), and an orchestra of fourteen pieces.

No doubt one could become hardened to sitting

all morning at one end of a parlor, gravely listening to the waltzes and two-steps of an orchestra
at the other, and after every selection even more
gravely adjourning with one's host and the musi-
cians to the dining room for a glass of cognac.
But there is about the first morning spent in this
fashion a ghastly charm. As the ladies did not take
cognac, upon them devolved the less invigorating
task of preserving unbroken during our frequent
absences the thread of conversation, and I groveled
before them in admiration every time I returned
and found that the children and the weather as
topics had not even begun to be exhausted. There
was all the more to say about the weather by reason
of the fact that there had been recently so little of
it—rain had refused to fall for weeks and the
coffee trees, laden with buds, were unable to flower.
With the crop in imminent peril—with hundreds
of thousands of dollars ready to dry up and blow
away all around us—we could still experience a kind
of social gratitude for the calamity, and toward
noon I began to feel that among the many kindly
acts of our host, his having had in all, six children
instead of only one or two was perhaps the kind-
liest. Race suicide on his part would have been
not only race suicide but conversational murder.

The eldest boy was at a Southern school in the United States, and (this, however, did not emerge during our visit; Don Juan perhaps did not know of it) he had on arriving, before the school opened, much to his amazement, been refused admittance, on account of his fine, dark skin (grandmamma was an Indian), to one hotel after another. The explanation of the person in charge of him to the effect that he was no more of African extraction than were the elegant young hotel clerks themselves, was unproductive of results.

"I don't care what he is—he isn't white," was their unanimous verdict, and he found refuge at last in an obscure boarding house. But apparently he had lived down prejudice even in the South, for while Don Juan was proud of the progress he had made in his studies, he was positively vain of his success with the ladies, although still somewhat at a loss to account for the state of affairs that rendered such admitted conquests possible. As modestly as he could he conveyed to us that the girls were "crazy" about Juanito, hastening to declare, as a parent should, that for his part he did not see precisely why.

"No doubt it is because Juanito is a novelty to them," he sought to explain. "You know how women are; always attracted by something new. On Sunday afternoons they take long walks with him—but all alone, *all alone.* No mother, father, brother—no one. And afterwards they invite him in to supper. But nothing wrong—nothing wrong " (Juanito was not quite fifteen), he added, closing his eyes and solemnly waving his finger in front of his face.

The dinner (it was announced at last) was a revelation in the possibilities of Mexican cooking, and although the multitude of dishes were not new to me their savor was. Grandmamma cooked from recipes (" muy, muy antiguas," they were) whose origins had been obscured by subsequent history, and almost a century had in no way impaired her sense of taste or her lightness of touch. Even her tortillas were delicious, and a tortilla is a melancholy form of nourishment. The mole (a turkey soaked in a rich, mahogany-colored sauce, composed of from twenty to half a hundred different ingredients) was of course the dinner's climax—it always is—and afterwards, as the old lady did not come to the table, we all went to the kitchen to congratulate her and shake her hand while the maids who had been helping her looked on in ecstasy.

" She doesn't come to the table because she has

only one tooth," her son explained as he gently caused her to display it, much as one exhibits the dental deficiencies of an old and well-beloved horse, " and on top there is no hair—none at all. You see—it's all bare, just like parchment. She's a wonderful woman," he declared, as he slid his finger back and forth on her skull.

Then we were shown the house; even—before we realized what was about to happen—the new bathroom, to whose undoubted conveniences Don Juan artlessly called out attention, and after examining separately every plant in the patio, we returned to the sala, where the darling weather proceeded almost immediately to save not only the situation but the coffee crop. A series of cloud-bursts kept us all at the open windows fascinated, as for some reason one always is by the hissing of rain and the violent activities of tin waterspouts, until their sudden cessation enabled us to stroll out, accompanied by Don Juan and the children, to visit the town's famous gardens for growing violets, azaleas, camelias, roses, and gardenias for the market. There did not seem to be many of them, but it was only later, when Don Pedro and his wife came to the train with their arms full, that we knew why.

In two hours the coffee had flowered, and as the

train lurched back to Barranca in the green, uncanny, storm-washed light, through acres and acres
and acres of white coffee blossoms, it was difficult
not to believe that there had been in the tropics a
fall of snow.

IX

IT is significant that the most entertaining as well as the most essentially true book on Mexico that I have been able to find was written during the years 1840 and 1841, by Madame Calderon de la Barca. Although from this name one does not, perhaps, at once jump to the conclusion that the writer was Scotch, the fact that she was becomes somewhat more credible on discovering her to have been born " Ingalls." She was, in a word, the wife of the first minister Spain condescended to send to Mexico after that dissatisfied country had, in the time-honored phrase, " thrown off the yoke," and she must have been a most intelligent and charming young person.

Of course, I have spent far too much time in and about Boston not to have observed that delightful books are often written by odious women, and what persuades me that my belief in Madame Calderon's charm is not misplaced is the fact that she never knew she was writing a book at all. " It consists of letters written to the members of her family, and really not intended originally — however incredible the assertion—for publication," says Prescott the historian, in his short preface to the volume. It was Prescott who urged her to print them, but even he could not induce her actually to reveal her name. I say "actually," as she resorted on the title page to the quaint form of anonymity that consisted of signing herself "Madame C— de la B—," a proceeding always suggestive of the manner in which the two-hundred-pound soprano of Mozart opera holds a minute, black velvet mask a foot and a half away from her face and instantly becomes invisible to the naked eye.

But what strikes me as significant when I open Madame Calderon's letters at random and read a page or two almost anywhere is that, while the book has long since been out of print, it is essentially not out of date. For although in sixty-six years many historical things have happened in Mexico — revolutions, sudden and astonishing changes of government, the complete and wonderful disestablishment of the Church, foreign invasions both bloody and peaceful — one may still read Madame Calderon and verify much that she says simply by glancing out of the window. Momentous changes have without doubt taken place: there are now freedom of religious belief and facilities for acquiring an education, where in her time there was only a priest with hell in one hand and a yawning purse in the other; there now are railways and an excellent post and telegraph service, where formerly there were, so to speak, nothing but brigands. The parents of an Englishwoman I know in Mexico, who as a young bride and groom landed at Vera Cruz just sixty years ago, were held up and robbed three times during their journey from the coast to Barranca. They were in a coach with other passengers, and the first bandits they encountered took merely their money. The second deprived them of their watches and jewelry, but the third, enraged at finding them without valuables of any kind, stripped everybody — including the driver — to the skin. Stark naked, the coachload for eight hours pursued its embarrassed way and stark naked it drove into the patio of the Barranca inn. To-day in Mexico one may occasionally be held up on the road, just as one may be held up in Wyoming or Vermont, but brigandage as a lucrative career for young men of courage has been suppressed. Madame Calderon did not seem to think it at all unlikely that the masked bandits who separated ladies from

their jewels on the way home from a ball at three
in the morning were the dashing army officers with
whom the ladies had been dancing and flirting a
short time before.

Those days are passed, and yet Mexico always
seems to me very much as it was when the ob-
servant Scotchwoman wrote her long and vivid letters. There have been "events," and reforms, and
innovations that unquestionably have had their influence on somebody, but the great masses appear
to have been quite uninfluenced. Even the large
towns—with the exception of the City of Mexico
and Guadalajara, both of which seem in many respects to become more cosmopolitan every week—
may still be recognized from Madame Calderon's
description of them and their inhabitants. As recently as this year (1908) it was impossible, at
the best hotel in Puebla (a capital with a population of at least a hundred thousand), to get
breakfast, if one was obliged to leave by the half-
past-six A.M. train for Jalapa.

"It is not the custom to serve breakfast so early,"
said the mozo, who was arranging my bed for the
night, when I ordered soft-boiled eggs and chocolate to be sent up at half past five for my mother
and brother and me. He was a handsome boy,

shivering in a dark-brown sarape stamped all over with white horseshoes.

"But my God, amigo mio!" I protested, "why *isn't* it the custom? Before a long journey even the most spiritual of us must fortify ourselves."

"The milkman does not come from the country until six," he then explained, "and the cook never lights the brasero until half past. Without milk and fire, how can one breakfast?"

To a person of resource (I am a person of resource) such a state of affairs is immaterial. For at half past five (with the ghastly before dawn cheerfulness that some of us at last painfully acquire) I was making my toilet with one hand and, on two alcohol lamps, boiling eggs and preparing chocolate with the other—as in Mexico I had done innumerable times before. But for the uninitiated and the resourceless—the American traveler in Mexico is usually both—what a situation!

A railway—an engineering marvel that in its construction again and again achieved the impossible—has bisected the country for almost thirty years; but I know many adult Mexicans of considerable intelligence, in their own circumscribed, tropical way, who have lived all their lives within sixty or seventy miles of the track without ever having seen

it. Sixty-six years ago France must have been decidedly more French, and Italy must have been
infinitely more Italian, than they are to-day, yet
Mexico apparently is but slightly less Mexican.

From Madame Calderon, and from her only, was
I able to learn the exact religious import of the nine
dances (posadas, they are called), given everywhere
in Mexico just before Christmas. I knew they were
given, for I had gone to them and enjoyed myself,
but just why there were nine of them and just why
they should all be held in quick succession immediately before Christmas, was something neither my
American nor my Mexican acquaintances—in spite
of their polite efforts to recollect a pretty legend,
they had forgotten — ever made altogether clear.
Madame Calderon, however, was more satisfactory,
and I can do no better than quote her: " This is the
last night of what are called the Posadas," she
writes, " a curious mixture of religion and amusement, but extremely pretty. The meaning is this:
At the time that the decree went forth from Cæsar
Augustus that ' all the world should be taxed,' the
Virgin and Joseph, having come out of Galilee to
Judæa to be inscribed for the taxation, found Beth-
lehem so full of people who had arrived from all
parts of the world that they wandered about for

nine days without finding admittance to any house or tavern, and on the ninth day took shelter in a manger, where the Savior was born."

"Posada" means an inn or lodging house, and the "curious" religious preliminaries to the nine dancing parties called "posadas" are all symbolical of the efforts of Joseph and Mary to find a resting place for the night. The posada Madame Calderon describes took place in a private house in the City of Mexico more than half a century ago; the last one I went to was held less than a year ago in the casino of a small town in the tierra templada. But except for some slight historical differences, either one might have been the other. "We went to the Marquesa's at eight o'clock, and about nine the ceremony commenced," writes Madame Calderon. And in this sentence lurks, perhaps, the greatest difference. For at the casino of Barranca I found no marquesas. Most of the pure-blooded Spaniards one meets in Mexico are either priests or grocers, and if any of them is a marqués—as is very possible—he has long ago tactfully pretended to forget it.

The casino at Barranca in itself throws some light on Mexican character. For a small town it is an elaborate structure—built about an impressive patio, with two large ballrooms and a supper room upstairs

and smaller rooms below for cards and billiard
tables. In England or in the United States these
ground-floor apartments would be adequately furnished, supplied with periodicals and newspapers, regarded as a man's club and used as such. But in
Mexico, a club, as we understand such an institution, seems, outside of the capital, to make little appeal. The satisfaction that Brown and Robinson
extract from reading their evening paper and sip-
ping their whisky-and-soda under a roof whose
shelter may not be sought by Smith and Jones, is a
satisfaction the Mexican in general has yet to discover. The reading room in the casino of Barranca
contains nothing to read, the billiard tables are
rarely played upon, and the card room is not often
occupied except on the night of a dance, when a
few middle-aged men whose wives and daughters
are upstairs in the ballroom endeavor to keep themselves awake over a mild game of poker. The truth
is that in Mexico the real clubs are the plaza and
the most centrally situated café. It is there that one
goes to read the paper, to smoke a cigar, to have
one's boots polished, to sit awhile on a bench and
talk to friends—to take a drink or have a game of
cards or billiards. It is there and not in the cold,
dreary rooms of the casino, that the gentlemen of

Barranca may usually be found when, for the moment, they haven't anything in particular to do. The plaza and the café are for every day; the casino is for occasions.

The greatest occasions are the nine posadas, all of which are exactly alike with the exception of the last, when a piñata (the grab-bag of one's childhood days) is suspended from the ceiling and finally induced to disgorge its treasures by a blindfolded young lady, who succeeds in demolishing it with a cane. On arriving, one is graciously received by an appallingly powdered reception committee, and when all the guests have assembled, partners are chosen, a procession is formed, everyone is given a lighted candle, the incandescent lamps are extinguished and, singing verse after verse that tells of the wanderings of Joseph and Mary, the party marches around and around the upper floor of the patio. When the night is clear and there is a moon, as happened to be the case at the last posada I went to, the performance, as Madame Calderon says, is " exceedingly pretty." Finally the procession stops in front of a closed door and sings, on the part of the Holy Family, a request for admittance. In an interesting change of key, a chorus of voices behind the door refuses to unlock. Mary and Joseph reply (always in song) that the night is cold and dark—the wind blows hard. Again they ask for shelter, and again they are refused. At this, Mary in a last verse reveals the fact that she is the Queen of Heaven—whereupon the door is instantly opened and the procession enters and disbands; not, however, before everyone has kissed a little image of the Infant Jesus reposing on a bed of leaves and flowers. After this ceremony—which no one seems to take at all seriously—the orchestra strikes up a two-step and the dance begins. Precisely this happens every evening—Sunday is an exception —for nine nights before Christmas, all over Mexico.

"Are there any girls you would like to meet?" inquired a Mexican friend of mine one evening, after Joseph and Mary had been admitted and the first dance was just beginning.

"Why, yes—introduce me to the tall girl in blue," I answered, indicating an aristocratic young person whose gown had rue de la Paix written all over it and who, in the matter of powder, combined Mexican quantity with Parisian art.

"Oh—she's the governor's daughter," my friend hesitated.

"Well, I care not who makes the daughters of a country, if I can make their acquaintance," I attempted to say in Spanish. It ended with my dancing several times with her, and I was much interested to note what an isolated and rather somber evening she spent. She was agreeable and beautifully dressed—but she was the governor's daughter, and the local youths for that reason were afraid of her and admired her at a distance. At an early hour she went home with her brother. He was the only person present in evening dress, and when he returned after escorting his sister home, he wore a frock coat. I have never been able to decide whether he made the change because he felt uncomfortable himself or because he wished to put the rest of us at our ease.

X

ONCE, in the United States I had to wait five hours for a train in a large prohibition town —a town that for many years has been a bright jewel in the Woman's Christian Temperance Union's crown of glory. As I was ignorant of this fact at the time, I asked one of the intellectual-looking waitresses at the hotel where I was eating my luncheon to bring me a bottle of beer. From the manner in which she snubbed me, I supposed the fair, pure city not only did not tolerate beer, but did not tolerate even the mention of beer. After luncheon, while I was sitting on the hotel piazza, I noticed that a great many men darted into an alley just opposite, passed through a doorway and never returned. As the hour grew later their numbers increased until the door was held open by an almost continuous stream. At times the room beyond the door apparently became so crowded that the men in the alley would form a long queue and patiently await their turn to enter. Thinking it might be a show of some sort, I made inquiries of a policeman,

158

who, much amused at my innocence, replied:
" Didn't you ever see a man take a drink before? "
Hundreds of men went in at the door during the
afternoon and emerged, it seemed, from a smug-
looking grocery store on another street. And everybody was satisfied: the good ladies of the Woman's
Christian Temperance Union, who apparently can
always be appeased by a bit of legislation; the inhabitants of the town, who drank as deep and as
often as they pleased. I was young at the time, and
although I have since discovered with much amusement and some gratification that the law which pre-
vents a man from obtaining a drink, when he really
wants one, has yet to be devised, the incident made
a lasting impression on me. I often recall my afternoon in the State of Maine, the alley, the little door,
the stream of men of every station in life.

In Mexico I have recalled it time and again, as
I gradually learned something about the theoretical
and the actual relations between the state and the
Church. For there is, on the one hand, precisely the
same stern attitude of the state toward religion
(which in Mexico really means Roman Cathol-
icism), and on the other the same official wink. In
1859 the great Benito Juarez proclaimed his highly
desirable Reform Laws, and in so doing simply

wiped from the slate the various complications that
had kept the clerical party and the liberal party,
from one end of the country to the other, in a state
of bloody war for fifty years. At one time every
public institution in Mexico was owned and managed by the Church. Every hospital, every school,
every asylum was church property. Even some of
the theaters were of religious origin. So great a
portion of the country's wealth was in the hands of
the priests that trade of all kinds was seriously hin-
dered. To some extent this state of affairs was alle-
viated even before the sweeping proclamation of
Juarez in 1859, but after it the claws of the Church
in Mexico seemed to be effectually extracted for all
time. All the remaining monastic orders were dis-
established by a stroke of the pen, and church property became national property. The cathedrals and
churches are now owned by the state and lent, so
to speak, to the Church for religious purposes. You
can't, according to the law, become a monk or a nun
in Mexico, even if you wish to; church bells may
not ring for more than one minute (I think it is
one minute) at a time, and priests may not either
wear, on the streets, a distinctively clerical costume
or, in a religious capacity, accompany a funeral to
the cemetery. (I confess that, although I believe

enthusiastically in every measure, however brutal, that effectively restrains the Lord's ambassadors from meddling in secular affairs, I have never been able to see the point of prohibiting a religious ceremony at a grave.) Once upon a time an English bishop who disembarked at Vera Cruz in the humorous costume to which his position in England entitled him, was, with a considerable flourish of trumpets, promptly arrested and compelled to change his clothes. The laws are there; they are extremely explicit, and now and then, as in the case of the English bishop, they are, for the pacification of the rabidly anticlerical, noisily enforced, but——

The President, in a word, is a person of great good sense, and I have gathered from the ultraclerical, profoundly monarchistic remarks of my friend Father O'Neil, who of course detests him, that in matters ecclesiastical he is inclined to let the letter of the law take care of itself. Father O'Neil doesn't know that I have derived any such impression from our long and interesting talks together, and I have never told him.

"Why is it the authorities don't arrest you?" I inquired of him one day when he had been holding forth on the indignities the Church was forever suffering at the hands of the Government. For he does not hesitate to appear on the streets in the whole paraphernalia.

"Ah, they will some day," he hopefully replied. And it was Father O'Neil also who told me that there were to-day between thirty and forty convents running full blast in the City of Mexico alone. That they are is against the law, but, after all, the channels through which they used to work great harm have been closed, and there are a number of persons in every community of human beings who are able to satisfy their temperamental needs—to enjoy life—only by walling themselves up with others similarly disposed and wearing garments of a particular shape and fabric. Once in so often the anticlericals explode quite in the manner of the Woman's Christian Temperance Union in the United States, declare that these illicit survivals must go, that such things must not be, and compel the police to make a raid. But the police, it is said, never discover anything on these expeditions beyond some demure ladies in ordinary dress, who do not appear to understand the sudden intrusion and who declare the place to be a poor but honest boarding house. When the police retire, the ladies get their veils and habits from the cellar where they have hidden them, put them on, and proceed with the life meditative, as before. That they are never taken unawares, Father O'Neil assures me, is due to the piety of the Señora Carmen Rubio de Diaz, the President's wife.

All of which helps one to believe that the President is a statesman and a diplomat—that he does not care if people swim, as long as they do not go too near the water. And that to be a successful president in Mexico is a task of considerable difficulty might be inferred from a trivial incident which took place some years ago. In receiving new envoys from foreign countries the President is invariably happy in the phrasing of his short speech of welcome—which, perhaps, does not seem altogether remarkable when one learns that he is always furnished with a copy of the newly arrived diplomat's extemporaneous remarks a week before they are delivered. On one occasion a foreign minister misguidedly undertook to improve upon his discourse between the time it had been submitted and approved and the hour at which he was officially received. With the best intentions he inserted several things that the President, who is distinctly " onto his job," would have quietly deleted had he seen them. The particular sentence that caused trouble was one in which the unsuspecting envoy invoked God to be prodigal of His blessings upon Don Porfirio's distinguished head. The anticlerical element—it can scarcely be called a party—was immediately incensed. It has a strong prejudice against God, and of the fact that the President had, as it were, officially recognized Him, it endeavored to make a political issue. The President was much annoyed by the affair, and the diplomat horrified. It has not happened again.

Father O'Neil is an American by way (on the part of his grandparents) of Ireland; but for many years he has been a Roman Catholic priest in Mexico, and he is one of those baffling, rather fascinating Roman Catholic enigmas that I have grown accustomed to meeting in lonely, far-away places. He is forty years old; a person of education, cultivated tastes, and great charm of manner. For years he was priest of a fever-stricken parish on the Isthmus of Tehuantepec until at last he got yellow fever himself and was obliged, in order to remain alive, to seek a higher altitude. When I knew him he was filling (at a salary of three hundred dollars a year) a quaint position in an isolated spot with a queer little history.

In the seventeenth century some Spanish monks founded a monastery in a very beautiful part of the great Mexican plateau. The monastery lasted—as an institution—for just a hundred years, at the end of which time, for reasons that do not appear in the records of the place, all the monks, with the exception of one, set sail for Spain. Those who left divided the money among them; the one who remained received the buildings and the land. He, by the Pope's dispensation, was permitted to marry, which he straightway did and begat a large family. His descendants have always owned the estate, and although the present members of the family do not live there, they still observe the wishes of the original owner by perpetually having a priest—a sort of family chaplain—in residence. When I met Father O'Neil, he was the chaplain. His entire duties consisted of saying eleven low masses a month (why eleven he did not know, except that this number had been stipulated for in the will of the late possessor) and taking care of the exquisite old vestments and gold service that dated from the place's founding. Very few persons ever went to the masses, and he confided in me that when absolutely no one was present he did not even pretend to say them. An agreeable man, a man of ability, fond of conversation, companionship, and good living.

"What fanatical zeal he must have," I at first

thought, " in order to exile himself to a locality that, however beautiful, is absolutely deficient in everything he so greatly enjoys." There were weeks at a stretch when he had no one to speak to but his mozo or the country folk who occasionally dropped in for the purpose of ascending the monastery's sacred stairs on their knees. Although interested in books and an acute critic of them, he had literally none.

" On three hundred a year one's library grows slowly," he once remarked to me. But as I came to know him better I discovered with amazement that he was not only not a devout man—he was one of the most essentially, innately irreligious persons I have ever met. The religious temperament and point of view—especially the Christian-religious point of view—bored him indescribably, and he usually spoke to me of his activities as a priest as if they were some sort of a tedious necessity. I saw him every few days for a whole winter, and in his long, cool, bare sala, adorned only with some of the monastic relics and a portrait of the monk who had remained in Mexico and founded the family, we discussed many things—but I never could manage to maintain a satisfactory discussion on the subject of *him*. When, for instance he would, in the most casual tone imaginable, exclaim: " Oh, by the way, don't write up any of those yarns I told you the other evening, as I got them all in the confessional," there were several leading questions I could have asked. For the fact that he could be amusing with the secrets of the confessional jarred even on me. But I never did. Once when I inquired if something or other had not surprised him, he replied: " My dear boy, I have belonged to three exceedingly illuminating professions: journalism, the law, and the Church; I am *never* surprised." Why had he left the first two, in either of which one could easily imagine him successful and happy, for the third, where he was neither one nor the other? And why was he buried alive in the interior of Mexico, endeavoring to exist on three hundred dollars a year, when he loved the world and candidly admitted that he enjoyed few things as much as he enjoyed spending money? I somehow hope I shall never find out.

Late one afternoon, when he was walking part of the way home with me, he stopped to have his hand kissed by an old Indian woman who kept a small cantina by the roadside. Doña Rosario invited us to have a drink at her expense, but insisted on serving it in a small inner room, rather than in the cantina proper, where half a dozen laborers were standing at the bar.

"I wouldn't ask the padrecito to drink with such common persons," she explained.

"But I don't mind, Doña Rosario," the priest assured her with a laugh. "We're all made of the same clay."

"So are cream pitchers and slop-jars; but they are not used for the same purposes," Doña Rosario prettily replied.

"Sometimes they *are*," he murmured to me in English as he swallowed his drink, and I've often wondered just what he meant.

XI

WHAT I am about to say will be of interest only to persons who for one reason or another are on the verge of a first trip to Mexico, as it will have to do chiefly with bald facts about the conditions of travel in the republic—railway trains, luggage, cabs, hotels, restaurants (there aren't any), baths, beds, bottled water, butter—anything indeed that occurs to me as relevant to the matter of travel. I know beforehand that my attempt to make a few practical, sensible remarks on the subject will prove unsatisfactory—perhaps exasperating. After one has lived in Mexico any length of time one completely forgets the point of view of persons who have never been there. So if I happen to leave out the one thing dear reader most wishes to be informed upon, I humbly hope I may be forgiven; for if I might choose between writing about such affairs and being broken on the wheel, I should immediately inquire the nearest way to the wheel. Suggestions as to routes of travel, excursions, and " sights," I omit deliberately, as all the Mexican railways publish attractive, illustrated folders that treat of these with much greater lucidity than I ever hope to attain.

Conventionally speaking, traveling in Mexico is uncomfortable. By this I don't mean that a person in ordinary health is subjected to hardships, but merely that trains and hotels always lack the pleasing frills to which one is accustomed in the United States and Europe. A train is a means of transporting yourself and your belongings from one place to another and nothing else. Americans—and with reason—look upon their best trains as this and considerably more. The Mexican cars follow the American plan of a middle aisle with exits at either end, and, as in Europe, are usually of the first, second, and third class. A first-class car resembles in every respect what is known in the United States as " a coach " (as distinguished from a sleeping and a parlor car)—even to its squalor. Furthermore, as there are rarely enough of them they are almost always crowded. I have often noticed that Mexicans, generally speaking, either can afford to travel first class, or can't afford to travel second. The second-class car is therefore sometimes comparatively empty and endurable when the other two are neither. Even after buying a first-class ticket I have more than once found it worth while to sit in a second-class car; but naturally this is not always true. Second-class cars for some reason are gradually being abolished.

In many of the larger places—the City of Mexico, Guadalajara, Puebla, Vera Cruz—you can buy tickets at the railway's city office and then at the station check luggage at any time. It is invariably a saving of good temper, anxiety, and comfort to do so, for the ticket window at the station (surrounded by a dense crowd of the unwashed) does not open until half an hour or twenty minutes before the train leaves, and it takes longer to check luggage in Mexico than in any country in which I have traveled. The system, in its final results, is precisely that of the United States; the things are weighed, one is charged for an excess of one hundred and fifty pounds on every first-class ticket, and given in some cases a separate cardboard check for every piece, and in others a printed, filled-in receipt for all of them on a slip of paper. But why so simple a process should take so much time I have not been able to learn. Recently in Vera Cruz it required at the station of the Interoceanico railway three quarters of an hour and the combined intellectual and physical efforts of two clerks and three cargadores (working hard all the time) to furnish me with checks for six trunks and several smaller pieces. Fortunately I had gone there long before train time and was the only passenger in the station. It is but fair to admit that there was a slight hitch in the proceedings—five or six minutes—when darkness overtook us before the electric light was turned on and some one had to rush out and buy a candle in order that work could be resumed (this in one of the great seaports of the world!), but all the rest of the time was consumed in checking the trunks. For each trunk they seem to write half a page of memoranda in a book, pausing now and then to lean back and look at the ceiling as if in the throes of composing a sonnet. All things considered, it is well in Mexico to allow yourself at the railway station what would seem in other countries a foolish amount of time.

In some of the towns most visited by tourists the trains are now met by English-speaking interpreters from the various hotels, who, by taking charge of the checks and baggage, make the arrival and departure of even persons who are new to the country and speak no Spanish a simple and painless matter. When this does not happen, however, you may put yourself with perfect confidence into the hands of a

licensed cargador—a licensed cargador being a porter
with a numbered brass tag suspended about his neck
on a string. Outside of the City of Mexico I have
never known a licensed cargador who was not, in
at least the practice of his profession, entirely capable and honest. He will carry your hand bags to a
cab, or in places where there are no cabs, to the
street car that invariably passes near the best hotels,
and a short time afterwards—if you have intrusted
him with your checks—arrive at the hotel with your
trunks. For carrying hand bags from the train to
the cab or street, twenty-five centavos is ample. The
charge for taking trunks from the station to the
hotel is usually fifty centavos apiece. As a measure
of absolute safety, although it is hardly necessary,
you may remove a cargador's tag from his neck and
keep it as a hostage until you receive your trunks.
A cargador with a license is for all reasons preferable to one without. Being licensed by the city
government, he has a definite status which he hesitates to imperil. By retaining his tag, or noting
and remembering his number, you have an infal-
lible means of identifying him in case your trunks
should fail to arrive. But they always do arrive.

Except in the City of Mexico you are rarely
tempted to get into a cab; you prefer either to walk

or to make use of the street cars which will always take you anywhere worth going to. In the capital, however, although the electric-car service is excellent, cabs seem to be a necessity. They are of two classes and the cost of riding in them is fixed by law, but unless you find out beforehand from some one who is informed upon the subject exactly how much you ought to pay, the cabman will demand several times his legal fare. On fête days and Sundays, and between the hours of midnight and six in the morning, the fare is double.

If your train leaves at an early hour in the morning, you cannot get breakfast at the hotels; coffee and rolls, or pan dulce—a slightly sweetened cross between bread and cake—is usually served somewhere in the station. There are no dining cars; the train instead stops at decent intervals at stations provided with clean and adequate Chinese restaurants. Even when the train is very late there is no need of being hungry; at almost every station women and girls walk up and down the platform selling fruit, pulque, and tortillas covered with strange, smeary condiments that taste much better than they look. One of these decorated tortillas and a glass of pulque may not exactly satisfy the appetite, but they effectually kill it. Pulque—a thin fluid re-

sembling water that has been poured into a recep-
tacle in which a little milk had been carelessly left—
tastes like a kind of degenerate buttermilk, and in
the middle of a hot journey is delicious and refreshing. It is derived from the sap of the maguey plant
and is often spoken of as " the national drink." This
somehow strikes me as a misnomer. Pulque is certainly peculiar to Mexico and on the highlands it
is drunk in enormous quantities. But in the tierra
caliente and the tierra templada where maguey does
not grow, what pulque there is has to be brought
from a distance and is neither good nor very popular.
In the lowlands fiery derivatives of the sugar cane
are much more prevalent. Although I have had
irrefutable ocular evidence to the effect that pulque,
when drunk in sufficient quantities, is extremely in-
toxicating, it is difficult after only a glass or two
to believe so. But I have drunk it only in the
country, where it is fresh and comparatively pure.
In towns it is invariably doctored and injurious.

If you are not too warm and too tired and too
cross, a Mexican railway journey is infinitely more
amusing than trips by rail elsewhere. In the first
place smoking, except in sleeping cars, is nowhere
prohibited, and smoking would tend to promote
sociability even if Mexicans on trains were not al-

ways eager to talk at any hour of the day or night. In a crowded car the volume of conversation is at times appalling. It is not perhaps deeply interesting, but it is always amiable, vivacious, and incessant, and if you show the slightest desire to participate you are never made to feel unwelcome.

The Anglo-Saxon shibboleth of travel is, I should say, neatness and reserve. We do not keep on adding to our carefully calculated luggage after we have once settled ourselves in a train, and we are not inclined to forsake our book or our magazine for a casual acquaintance unless we have some reason to believe the exchange will be profitable. Mexicans, on the other hand, are in an engaging fashion the most slovenly and expansive little travelers imaginable. For laden though they be with all manner of flimsy baggage, they impulsively buy everything that is thrust at them—if it takes up enough room and is sufficiently useless—and talk to everyone in sight.

The train, for instance, stops at a lonely station in a vast dun-colored plain, planted everywhere in straight, never-ending lines of maguey. At the foot of the bare mountains in the distance, and seen through a faint haze of dust, is the high white inclosure around the buildings of an hacienda with the tiled dome and towers of its private church glitter-

176

ing in the sunlight. Two antique, high-hung carriages with dusty leather curtains, each drawn by a pair of mules, are at one side of the station, and standing near by a neat mozo, with a smart straw sombrero (a Mexican hat, more than other hats takes on something of the nature of its owner), and a narrowly folded red sarape reposing—Heaven knows how; I can't carry one that way—on his left shoulder, is holding three saddle horses. The antique carriages—they look as if they dated from the time of Maximilian, and probably do—have brought the hacendado, his imposing wife, two babies, three older children, a nurse for each baby, and two dressy, hatless young ladies, from the house to the train. One of the horses was ridden by a mozo who is to accompany the family on its travels (he, however, goes second class), the second brought the mozo who is to lead back the horse of the first, while the third— a finer animal who objects to trains and whose head has been left tightly checked for the benefit of the passengers—carried a slender young man, presumably the son, who has come to see the others off. Mamma is not yet middle-aged, but her figure—her waist line—is but a reminiscence; has passed in fact into Mexican history. She wears a heavy brown woolen skirt (the thermometer stands at about 92°),

a rebozo twisted around her arms and across her
back as if she were a lady Laocoon, and a shirt waist
of white cashmere covered with large crimson polka
dots; the kind of material that makes one feel as if
a very methodical person had had the nose-bleed.
Papa has on skin-tight trousers of shepherd's plaid,
a " boiled " shirt with a turned-over collar (clean—
but they wilted on the drive), a plain black jacket
that extends only a few inches below his belt, a
flowing silk necktie of the peculiarly beautiful shade
of scarlet one usually sees in the neckties of rurales,
a small but businesslike revolver in a holster at his
hip, and a shaggy, gray beaver sombrero embroidered
around the brim in gold and silver flowers, weigh-
ing about two pounds and costing at least seventy-
five or a hundred pesos. The older children—little
girls—and the two dressy, hatless young ladies are
in what might be called the Franco-Mexican style
of traveling costume; thin summer dresses of bright
pink and yellow and blue and white materials made
with many little tucks and frills and ruffles, and
adorned with narrow bands of coarse white lace
applied in a rather irrelevant fashion with here and
there a knot of soiled white satin ribbon. Besides a
goodly number of venerable valises they have brought
with them the usual collection of cardboard hat

boxes and tenates (a kind of flexible basket without handles, made of matting). Some of their effects are informally wrapped in bath towels of pleasing hues. It takes much time, a whirlwind of talk and all the remaining space in the car, to stow away everybody and everything; then as the train moves from the station there is a shrill chorus of good-bys and a prolonged wiggling of fingers through the windows at the son on the platform.

As it is only two o'clock in the afternoon, they undoubtedly were fortified by an elaborate midday meal about an hour and a half before, but at the next station oranges are offered for sale, so papa through the window buys a dozen oranges and everybody, maids and all—except the youngest baby— eats one. A few stations farther on we pass through a kind of an oasis where flowers are grown for the market. Short sections of the trunk of a banana tree, hollowed out, stopped at both ends and filled with gardenias, are held up to the window. Everyone exclaims, " Oh que bonitas! " and as they have more things now than they can take care of, mamma buys one of them and, after a short mental struggle, the elder of the dressy young ladies buys another.

" How fragrant they are! " you murmur as the sweet, opaque scent of the gardenias begins to join forces with the tobacco smoke and the lingering smell of the eleven oranges. Papa, delighted, at once picks out one of the largest flowers and hands it to you across the aisle. Your thanks are profuse and there is a moment of intensely interested silence while you smell it and put it in your button-hole. Then you ask mamma what they are called in Spanish, and after she tells you—repeating the name emphatically four or five times—she asks you if they grow in your country. You reply yes, but that they are expensive—costing in midwinter sometimes as much as a dollar gold apiece. This announcement creates a tremendous sensation on the part of everyone, as mamma didn't pay a fifth of that sum for all of them. One of the dressy young ladies says she is going to count hers to see how much they would come to in the United States in midwinter; and now the bark of conversation having been successfully launched, you sail pleasantly along in it until the next station, where one of the three little girls interrupts with the exclamation that on the platform she sees some papayas. A papaya being a bulky, heavy fruit of irregular shape and the size of a large squash, papa naturally leans out of the window and acquires two—buying the second one, he explains, in case he should be disappointed in the flavor of the first. But before the opening of the papaya you excuse yourself and go into another car, for without a plate and a knife and a spoon, a papaya, like a mango, can be successfully managed only while naked in a bath tub. After it is all over, however, you return for more talk, and for days afterwards, if your destination happens to be the same, you and papa wriggle fingers at each other from passing cabs, and you and mamma and the two dressy young ladies (who still haven't hats) bow as old friends. But about hotels——

They are, broadly speaking, of three kinds. First, the ordinary "best hotel" and next best hotel of the place, conducted by Mexicans who have gradually made concessions to progress until their establishments are equipped with electric lights, electric bells (sometimes), sanitary plumbing, wire-spring mattresses (or whatever they are called), some comfortable chairs in either the patio or the sala, and cooks whose dishes, although native in conception, are yet conservative in the matter of chile and lard. Secondly, there is the occasional hotel kept by an American family, whose advertisements emphasize the fact that here you will enjoy the delights of "American home cooking." And, finally, there is what is known in

Mexico as a mesón: a combination of lodging house for man and stable for his horses and mules.

The ordinary best and second-best hotels in Mexican towns I have grown to regard as exceedingly creditable and satisfactory places in which to abide. They are not luxurious; tiled floors, with a strip of carpet or matting at the bedside, calcimined walls without pictures, just sufficient furniture, and high, austere ceilings, are not our idea of luxury. But as long as they preserve their distinctly Mexican characteristics they are, contrary to the conventional idea of the country, above all, clean. I have rarely been in a Mexican hotel where the chambermaids (who are usually men) did not all but drive me insane with their endless mopping and dusting and scouring and polishing of my ascetic bedroom. When, however, as sometimes happens, the proprietor of the "best" hotel becomes desirous of upholstered chairs and carpets, it is well, I think, to patronize the still Mexican second best. Few things are more lovable than carpets and upholstery worn shabby by those we care for, but nothing is more squalid and repulsive than the evidence of unknown contacts paid for by the day or week. The hotels, as a rule, are of two stories built around a tiled patio, full of flowers and plants, and open to the sky. The more expensive rooms have windows looking upon the street, and in cold or gloomy weather have the advantage of being lighter and warmer than the others. In very hot weather, however, the cheap rooms—dim, windowless, and opening only on the patio—are sometimes preferable. Prices vary slightly in different places and at different seasons, but at their highest they are never really exorbitant, outside of the Capital. Board and lodging costs anywhere from two and a half to five pesos a day, according to the situation of your room, and, unlike European hotels, this includes everything. There are none of the extra charges for light, attendance, "covers," and so on, that in Europe so annoy the American traveler. At one hotel at Cuernavaca, during the tourist season, rooms and board are as high as six pesos a day, but this lasts only a short time, and is, after all, not so ruinous as it sounds when you think of it as three American dollars rather than six Mexican pesos. For a peso or so less you can, if you wish, take a room at a hotel without board; but unless you happen to have friends in town who keep house, and with whom you constantly lunch and dine, there is no advantage in doing so, as the best restaurant is invariably that of the best hotel.

When I said that there were no restaurants in Mexico, I merely meant that while the various native fondas and cafés where meals are served are sometimes clean and adequate, they do not offer any of those attractions that in the cities of Europe, and a very few cities of the United States, tempt one from one's ordinary existence. There is in Mexico no "restaurant life" (for want of a better term), no lavishly appointed interiors where you may go to watch well-dressed people spending a great deal of money, listening to music, and eating things they are unaccustomed to at home.

The meals in Mexican hotels are: Breakfast, from about seven to half past nine, consisting of coffee, chocolate, or tea, and pan dulce or rolls. Eggs and meat are extra. To a few teaspoonfuls of excessively strong coffee is added a cupful of boiling milk. Mexican coffee is excellent in itself, but the native habit of overroasting it makes its flavor harsh. As milk is almost always boiled in Mexico, cream is unknown. Chocolate is good everywhere, although it is difficult at first to reconcile yourself to the custom, in some places, of flavoring it with cinnamon. Persons who like tea for breakfast, or at any time, should travel with their own.

At dinner—from noon to about half past two—
you are given soup, sometimes fish, eggs always
(cooked in any way you please), meat (beefsteak
or roast beef), chicken (or another kind of meat),
with salad if you ask for it, frijoles (a paste of
black beans), a desert (preserves of some sort,
rarely pastry), fruit, and coffee. All of which
sounds rather better than it ever is. The dinner
is served in courses, and in some hotels you are
expected to use the same knife and fork throughout. You never have any desire to eat or, after
the first day or so, to try everything. The soups
are well flavored and nourishing, the eggs are always fresh, the frijoles preserve a certain standard
throughout the country, which you appreciate if
you like frijoles, either the chicken or one of the
meats is as a rule possible—and after all, soup,
eggs, frijoles, another vegetable, a meat, lettuce,
and fruit ought to be enough. The hard rolls you
get everywhere are of good quality and well baked.
Butter, fortunately, is almost nonexistent, as it is
very bad. The only edible butter in Mexico is
made in Kansas, and can be bought in convenient
one-pound packages at the leading grocery stores
in the City of Mexico, and also in some of the
smaller towns. There is no objection whatever to

your taking your own tea and butter, or anything
else that contributes to your comfort, into the
dining room of Mexican hotels. Except during
the hours at which meals are served, you cannot
get anything to eat. Persons who are accustomed
to some form of refreshment before going to bed
should keep it in their rooms.

Supper—from half past six until about nine
o'clock—is, except for the omission of eggs, very
much like dinner, although somewhat less elaborate in small places. (I employ the terms dinner
and supper rather than luncheon and dinner, as
they are the literal translations of the Spanish
words comida and cena.)

"Don't monkey with Mexican microbes! A
stitch in time may save six weeks in the hospital!
Let the other fellow run the risk of typhoid, if
he wishes to!"—so runs, in part, the advertisement
of a certain bottling company in Mexico. The fact
that the advice is primarily intended to increase
the sales of the firm in question does not render
it the less sound. Mexicans are peculiarly ignorant of the principles of sanitation, and careless of
them even when informed. Typhus, typhoid, and
smallpox are prevalent in the City of Mexico all
the year round, although, either through indiffer-

ence or a reluctance to admit it, cases are not reported in the newspapers until the frequency of funerals begins to cast a universal gloom. Impure water may or may not have any bearing upon typhus and smallpox; upon typhoid, however, it has. In many of the smaller towns the water, brought as it is in pipes from a distance, is pure and healthful, but you cannot be sure of just what happens to it after it has arrived. It is far more prudent, unless you are keeping house and can boil water, to drink a pure, bottled mineral water. The most convenient—for the simple reason that it can be bought at almost any bar from end to end of the country—is the Tehuacan water (Agua Tehuacan) bottled at Tehuacan by several companies; the San Lorenzo, the Cruz Roja, and El Riego, the chemical analysis of all the waters being about the same. It is light, refreshing, absolutely pure, and bottled by machinery with every precaution. The water from the Cruz Roja spring, in fact, is not even exposed to the air from the time it enters a pipe underground to when it is forced, a moment later, into a bottle and sealed.

Few beds in Mexico have arrived at the sybaritic luxury of feather pillows. The national pillow is a narrow, long, unsympathetic contrivance tightly stuffed with hair, or something more unyielding. You should travel with your own pillow, and also with a blanket or a steamer rug. Also, few hotels have facilities for bathing. To take a bath, one goes out to a bathing establishment (there are always several), where hot and cold water, clean towels, and soap are plentiful and cheap. As the Anglo-Saxon cold bath has little relation to cleanliness, and is merely either an affectation on the part of persons who don't enjoy it or a pleasant shock to the system on the part of those who do, it may be dispensed with or taken in a basin.

At night, hotels lock their massive front doors at ten or half past, but a porter sleeping on the floor just inside admits you at any hour. All over the world, servants like to be tipped, and the custom of tipping obtains in Mexico as elsewhere, but as yet it has remained within decent bounds. A mozo in a Mexican hotel is pleased, and sometimes surprised, by what his European or American equivalent would probably scorn.

To make a point of such trivial matters as matches, candles, keys, and door knobs will probably seem as if I were going out of my way, but in Mexico I have been the amused witness of so much real anguish occasioned by the presence or absence of these prosaic implements that in regard to them I feel a certain responsibility. Almost everywhere there are incandescent lights in Mexican hotels, but in some places the power is turned off at midnight, or half an hour later, and, as happens in all countries, the lights, at inopportune moments now and then, go out. When they do go out, you grope helplessly in darkness, for it is not customary to foresee such emergencies and supply the bedrooms with matches and candles. A candle and a box of matches in your traveling bag may never be needed, but when they are needed they are needed instantly, and you will be glad you have them. Door knobs in Mexico, for absolutely no reason whatever, are placed so near the frame of the door that it is almost impossible to grasp them without pinching your fingers, and in order to lock or unlock a door the key, as a rule, must be inserted upside down, and then turned the wrong way.

The following notice (it hung, printed and framed, in the sala of a Mexican hotel) will, I feel sure, prove of interest to the student of language:

"It is not permitted for any whatsoever motive to use this saloon to eat, or for games of ball or others that could prejudice the tranquillity of the passengers, or furthermore to remove the furnitures from their respective sites. At eleven of the clock the Administrador will usurp the right to order the extinguishment of the lamp without permitting of observations."

The second kind of hotel (the hotel kept by an American) possesses the various defects of a Mexican establishment, with several others all its own. It is rarely as clean as a Mexican hotel, and the "home cooking" so insisted upon in the advertisements merely means that the cooking is of the kind the proprietress was accustomed to before her emigration—which does not necessarily recommend it. "American cooking" or "home cooking" is no better than any other kind of cooking when it is bad. You don't eat through sentiment or patriotism, but through necessity. Among this class of hotel I feel it is only honest to except one at Cuernavaca, which has charming rooms, a most exquisite patio, and an "American table" about as good as that of the average New England summer boarding house.

Few Americans who are traveling for pleasure in Mexico will be likely to patronize what is known as a mesón. It would not have occurred to me to do so had I not slept in them in small towns off the

line of the railway, where there is no place else to
stay. When traveling on a horse or a mule, a
night's lodging for the steed is, of course, even more
essential than for the rider, and the mesón, as I
have said, is a combination of inn and stable.
Primitive and comfortless as they often are, they
have for me a fascination—the fascination of something read and thought of in childhood that in later life suddenly and unexpectedly comes true. A
Mexican mesón, with its bare little bedrooms on
one side of the great courtyard and its stalls for the
animals on the other; with its clatter of arriving
and departing mule trains, its neighing and bray-
ing and shoeing and currying, its litter of equipment and freight—saddles, bridles, preposterous
spurs, pack saddles, saddle bags, saddle blankets,
conical sugar loaves and casks of aguardiente from
some sugar hacienda, boxes, bales, sacks of coffee—
its stiff and weary travelers, its swearing, swag-
gering arrieros—it is the Spain of the story-books,
the Spain of Don Quixote. You fall asleep at an
early hour to the rhythmic crunching of mules'
teeth on cane leaves and corn, and you are awak-
ened in the cold dark by the voice of your mozo
slowly and solemnly proclaiming: "Señor, es de
dia." (It is day.)

I perhaps should not have mentioned the mesón if its attraction for me had not led me to try it in cities where there was no necessity to. Even in the cities and large towns it is still a primitive institution, but it is always inexpensive, and the rooms in those of the better class are clean. I have had a well-lighted room of ample size, with a comfortable bed, a washstand, a table, two chairs, a row of hooks to hang clothes on, and an attentive mozo usually within call, for seventy-five centavos (thirty-seven and a half cents) a day. There are no restaurants attached to these places, and absolutely no one in them speaks English.

In fact, although Mexicans are becoming more and more interested in English, and are everywhere studying the language, it is as yet not very coherently spoken by the natives with whom a traveler is likely to come in contact. A few sentences by a clerk in a shop, half a dozen disconnected words by a waiter in a hotel, are about the extent of what you hear among the working classes. And yet, with no knowledge of Spanish, you can, without mishap or difficulty, travel by rail almost anywhere in Mexico. The country is accustomed to travelers who do not speak its language, and more often than not knows instinctively and from habit what they want next. Of course, to be able to ask questions and understand the answers is both a convenience and a pleasure; but it is surprising how far a very few words of Spanish on the one hand and English on the other will carry you in comparative peace of mind. When the worst comes to the worst, as by an unforeseen combination of circumstances it sometimes does, and you are on the point of losing your reason or, what is much worse, your temper, the inevitable kind lady or kind gentleman, who is to be found in every country and who knows everything, always appears at the proper moment, asks if he can be of any assistance, and sends you on your way rejoicing. In any event, in provincial Mexico nothing unpleasant is likely to happen to you.

Just what is the attitude toward foreigners of the people in general it is difficult—impossible, even—to find out. A year or so ago, several weeks before the 16th of September (the anniversary of Hidalgo's Declaration of Independence), it was widely announced in the newspapers of the United States that far-reaching plans had been laid by the lower classes in Mexico to observe the national festival by killing all foreigners. "Mexico for Mexicans" was to be the motto of the future. This quaint conceit—evolved, without doubt, by the pestiferous revolutionary junta in Saint Louis—was not much heard of by foreigners in Mexico; but then, in Mexico very little *is* heard of. A few timid persons remained at home during the day, but the day passed off without bloodshed, and the rumor was decided to have been only a rumor. That there was, however, more to it than was generally supposed (although how much more it would be impossible to find out) was evident from the fact that the Government quietly and inconspicuously took notice of it. In one place, where I have some American friends living on the edge of town —almost in the country—two rurales, heavily armed as usual, sauntered out to their houses at an early hour of the morning, and remained there all day and until late that night. As they spent the time in chatting and smoking with acquaintances who happened to pass by, it was not obvious that they were there for any especial purpose. But they were there, although they had never been there before and have never been there since. In another town a group of noisy hoodlums went at night to the house of one of the consuls (not the Spanish consul, by the way, which would have been more or less natural) with the intention of " doing something," just what, they themselves apparently did not know. Here, also, were two rurales, and at sight of them the intentions of the little mob prudently underwent a collapse. The spokesman soon summoned sufficient courage to request that they please be allowed to break a few windows if they promised to go no farther, but the rurales replied that the first man who even stooped to pick up a stone would be shot. Whereupon the crowd retired. (It is irrelevant, but also amusing, to record that on the retreat the members of the gang got into a quarrel among themselves, during which two of them were stabbed and killed.) Beyond an admirable preparedness on the part of the Government, this proves little, as the consul in question was personally most unpopular with the people of the town. But it of course proves something—or the Government wouldn't have been so prepared—although I find it difficult to see in it a proof of hostility toward foreigners on the part of the great mass of the Mexican people. If they do feel unkindly toward us, they are adepts in prolonged and continuous deception, for they are universally responsive to friendly overtures.

On the whole, I should not advise an invalid to go to Mexico, for I have met invalids there who,

although they perhaps might not have been happy
anywhere, struck me as being for many unavoidable
reasons more unhappy in Mexico than they would
have been had they sought a warm climate nearer
home.   There are a few enchanting places in Mexico where the weather is warm and reasonably equa-
ble all winter, but very few.   And when Mexico
is cold, it is dreary even for the robust.   Its
changes of temperature are sudden and penetrating,
and, except in one or two hotels in the capital
(an impossible place for invalids of any kind), artificial heat is practically unknown.   The problem
of simple, nourishing food is an insoluble problem
unless you keep house; only by exercising self-
restraint as regards Mexican cooking can well persons remain well.   There are no hotels that in the
slightest degree take into consideration the needs,
the whims, the capricious hours, the endless exi-
gencies of the sick, and anyone whose well-being
is dependent upon warm rooms, good milk, quiet
(the country is incessantly noisy with the noise of
animals and bells and human beings), or upon all
or any of the little, expensive niceties of modern
civilization, had better indefinitely postpone his
visit.

XII

A FEW days ago a friend of mine in writing to me from home said in his letter: " I notice that now and then you refer casually to ' an American man ' or ' an English woman who lives here,' and although I know there must be Americans and English living in Mexico as well as everywhere else, it always gives me a feeling of incredulity to hear that there are. I suppose I ought merely to consider the fact that you are there and then multiply you by a hundred or a thousand—or ten thousand perhaps; I have no idea, of course, how many. But to tell the truth I never altogether believe that *you* go to Mexico when you say you do. You go somewhere, but is it really Mexico? Why *should* anyone go to Mexico? It seems such a perverse—such a positively morbid thing to do. And then, the address—that impossible address you leave behind you! Honestly, are there any Americans and English down there (or is it ' up ' or ' across ' or ' over '—I literally have forgotten just where it is), and if so, why are they

197

there? What are they like? How do they amuse themselves?"

When I read his letter I recalled an evening several years ago at my brother's coffee place—sixty miles from anywhere in particular. As it was in winter, or the "dry season," it had been raining (I don't exaggerate), with but one or two brief intermissions, for twenty-four days. In that part of the republic the chief difference between the dry season and the rainy lies in the fact that during the rainy season it rains with much regularity for a few hours every afternoon and during the dry season it rains with even greater regularity all the time. As the river was swollen and unfordable we had not been able for days to send to the village—an hour's ride away—for provisions. Meat, of course, we did not have. In a tropical and iceless country, unless one can have fresh meat every day, one does not have it at all. We had run out of potatoes, we had run out of bread (baker's bread in Mexico is good everywhere)—we had run out of flour. There were twenty-five or thirty chickens roosting on a convenient tree, but in our foolish, improvident way we had allowed ourselves to become fond of the chickens and I have an incorrigible prejudice against eating anything that has engaged my affections when in life. So we dined on a tin of sardines, some chile verde and a pile of tortillas, which are not bad when patted thin and toasted to a crisp. Probably because there were forty thousand pounds of excellent coffee piled up in sacks on the piazza, we washed down this banquet with draughts of Sir Thomas Lipton's mediocre tea. The evening was cold—as bitterly cold as it can be only in a thoroughly tropical country when the temperature drops to forty-three and a screaming wind is forcing the rain through spaces between the tiles overhead. We had also run out of petroleum, and the flames of the candles on the dinner table were more often than not blue and horizontal. But somehow we dined with great gayety and talked all the time. I remember how my brother summoned Concha the cook, and courteously attracted her attention to the fact that she had evidently dropped the teapot on the untiled kitchen floor—that the spout was clogged with mud and that it did not " wish to pour," and how he again summoned her for the purpose of declaring that the three dead wasps he had just fished out of the chile no doubt accounted perfectly for its unusually delicious flavor. We had scarcely anything to eat, but socially the dinner was a great success. Immediately afterwards we both went to bed—each with a reading candle, a book and a hot-water bag. After half an hour's silence my brother irrelevantly exclaimed:

"What very agreeable people one runs across in queer, out-of-the-way places!"

"Who on earth are you thinking of now?" I inquired.

"Why, I was thinking of *us*!" he placidly replied, and went on with his reading.

Perhaps we had been agreeable. At any rate we were in a queer out-of-the-way place, that is if any place is queer and out of the way, which I am beginning rather to doubt. Since then I have often remembered that evening—how, just before it grew dark, the tattered banana trees writhed like gigantic seaweed in the wind, and the cold rain hissed from the spouts on the roof in graceful, crystal tubes. Here and there the light of a brazero in a laborer's bamboo hut flared for an instant through the coffee trees. On the piazza, the tired Indians, shivering in their flimsy, cotton garments, had covered themselves with matting and empty coffee sacks and were trying to sleep. In the kitchen doorway a very old, white-bearded man was improvising poetry—sometimes sentimental, sometimes heroic, sometimes obscene—to a huddled and enthralled audience all big hats, crimson blankets, and beautiful eyes. Apart from this group, Saturnino was causing a jarana to throb in a most syncopated, minor, and emotional fashion. A jarana is a primitive guitar whose sounding board consists usually of an armadillo's shell. (Poor Saturnino! He is now in indefinite solitary confinement for having, apropos of nothing except a slip of a girl, disemboweled one of his neighbors with a machete. And he was such a gentle, thoughtful creature! I don't quite understand it.) During dinner we discussed, among other things, Tolstoi's "War and Peace" which we had just finished, and while agreeing that it was the greatest novel we had ever read or ever expected to read (an opinion I still possess), we did not agree about Tolstoi's characteristically cocksure remarks on the subject of predestination and freedom of the will. As neither of us had studied philosophy we were unable to command the special terminology—the specific jargon that always makes a philosophic discussion seem so profound, and our colloquial efforts to express ourselves were at times piquant. In the midst of it a tarantula slithered across the tablecloth and I squashed him with a candlestick as he was about to disappear over the table's edge. Of course we disputed as to whether or not, in the original conception of the universe, God had sketched the career of the tarantula in its relation to that of the candlestick and mine, and—yes, on looking back, I feel sure we were both very agreeable.

But what I imagine I am trying to get at is that I have so often wonderingly contrasted the general scene with our being there at all, and then have remembered the simple, prosaic circumstances that had placed us in the midst of it. In a way, it is a pity one *can* remember such things; the act renders it so impossible to pose to oneself as picturesque. And, furthermore, it tends to shake one's belief in the picturesqueness of one's American and English acquaintances. (Perhaps I mean " romance " rather than picturesqueness, for compared to the fatuity of importing picturesqueness into Mexico, the carrying of coals to Newcastle would be a stroke of commercial genius.) At first there seems to be something romantic about all of one's compatriots who live in small Mexican towns, or on far-away ranches, plantations, fincas, haciendas — or whatever their property happens to be called. To the newly arrived there is a sort of thrill merely in the fashion in which they take their florid, pictorial environment for granted. I shall not forget my first New Year's Day in Mexico.

VIVA MEXICO!

Until the day before, I had never been in the country, and there was something ecstatic in the vividness of not only the day as a whole, but of every detail of color, form, temperature, personality, and conversation. It seemed as if everything in turn leaped out and seized hold of me, and now, long afterwards, I recall it as one of those marvelous days without either half tones or perspective, on which every separate fact is brilliant, and all are of equal importance. Only once since then has Mexico had just the same memorable effect upon me, and that was one night in the little plaza of Jalapa when, as the front doors of the cathedral swung open and the crowd within swarmed down the steps in the moonlight, the band abruptly crashed into the bull-fightingest part of " Carmen."

In the tepid, springlike afternoon I pushed back a five-barred gate, and through a pasture, where horses stopped grazing to snuff at me, over a wall of piled stones covered with heliotrope, I strolled up between banana trees to a yellow, stucco-covered house on the hillside. The way to the piazza was through a tunnel of pale-yellow roses with pink centers and on the piazza was an American lady, an American gentleman, a great many languorous-looking chairs, and two gallons of eggnog in a bowl of

Indian pottery. All of the small Anglo-Saxon colony
and a few others had been asked to drop in during
the afternoon, but I was the first to arrive, and I
remember that the necessary interchange of commonplace civilities with my hosts, the talk of mutual acquaintances on the boat from New York and
the answering of questions about weather and politics in the United States, seemed unspeakably shallow to one suddenly confronted by so exquisite and
sublime a view. For the view from the piazza, I
hasten to add by way of justifying two words so
opposite in suggestion, was, I afterwards learned,
characteristic of the mountainous, tropical parts of
Mexico, and, like most of the views there, combined
both the grandeur, the awfulness of space and height
—of eternal, untrodden snows piercing the thin
blue, with the soft velvet beauty of tropical verdure
—the unimaginable delicacy and variety of color
that glows and palpitates in vast areas of tropical
foliage seen at different distances through haze and
sunlight. Mountains usually have an elemental,
geologic sex of some sort, and the sex of slumbering, jungle-covered, tropical mountains is female.
There is a symmetry, a chaste volcanic elegance
about them that render them the consorts and
daughters of man-mountains like, say, the Alps, the

Rockies, the mountains of the Caucasus. At their cruelest they are rarely somber; their precipitous sides and overhanging crags are sheathed in vegetation of a depth that refines and softens, and the quivering lights and shadows that at times are apparently all their substance, are the lights and shadows of those excessively etherealized, vignetted engravings on the title pages of old gift books.

At the sloping pasture's lower end the compact, tile-roofed, white-walled town glared in the January sunlight—a town in a garden, or, when one for a moment lost sight of the outlying orange groves, fields of green-gold sugar cane, patches of shimmering corn and clumps of banana trees—an all-pervasive garden in a town. For compact as the Oriental-looking little place was, green and purple, yellow and red sprang from its interstices everywhere as though they had welled up from the rich plantations below and overflowed. One gazed down upon the trees of tiny plazas, the dense dark foliage of walled gardens, into shady, flower-filled patios and sunny, luxuriant, neglected churchyards, and beyond, the mysterious valley melted away in vast and ever vaster distances—the illimitable valley of a dream—a vision—an allegory—slowly rising at last, in tier upon tier of faintly opalescent volcanoes, the texture of gauze. Up and up and up they lifted and swam and soared, until, as with a swift concerted escape into the blue and icy air of heaven, they culminated in the smooth, inaccessible, swan-like snow upon the peak of Orizaba. Mexico's four, well-defined climates, from the blazing summer of the valley, to glittering winter only some thousands of feet above, were here, I realized, all the year round, visibly in full blast.

Then other guests began to push back the heavy gate and stroll up the long slope, and I found myself meeting them and hearing them all talk, with a thrill as keen—if of a different quality—as that with which I had gaped at the view. They seemed to me then quite as unreal. There was about them an impenetrable aura of fiction; they were the plain tales that Kipling would have lashed to the mast had his hills been Mexican—had Simla been Barranca.

There was the British consul—a quaint, kindly, charming little man—who while in the act of delightedly making one pun could scarcely conceal the eagerness and anxiety with which his mind grappled with the problem of how to introduce the next. The French consul, too, was of the gathering, and I don't know why, but life, somehow, would not have

seemed what it was that day if the French consul
had not been unmistakably a German. He had
brought with him a bouquet of pretty daughters
whose English accent and complexions (their mother
was English) and French deportment made of them
rather fascinating racial enigmas. Mrs. Belding
liked the girls but confided to me that in general
she considered the foreign manner all "French
jeune filledlesticks." Mrs. Hammerton, a tall, dis-
tinguished-looking, dark-haired English woman of
thirty, was perishing—so Mrs. Belding almost at
once informed me—for a cigar. She had an aged
mother, had had a romance (of which no one spoke,
declared Mrs. Belding as she spoke of it), and
adored Mexican cigars. Almost immediately upon
my meeting her she let me know in the prettiest, most
cultivated of voices that Mrs. Belding was in the
habit of getting tight.

There were two reasons for Mrs. Hammerton's
postponing just then the longed-for cigar. One was
the Rev. Luke M. Hacket, and the other was his
wife. Mr. and Mrs. Hacket, with an ever-growing
band of little Hackets, had lived for years at Barranca at the expense of many worthy and unintel-
ligent persons at home. They were there, all unconscious of their insolence, for the purpose of trying

to seduce Roman Catholics away from their belief
and supplying them with another; of substitu-
ting a somewhat colorless and unmagnetic expression of the Christian idea for one that satisfies not
only some of the Mexican's alert senses, but his
imagination as well. That these efforts at conver-
sion met with scarcely any success except during a
few weeks before Christmas (after which there was
always an abrupt stampede to Rome), did not much
concern them as long as Mrs. Hacket's lectures in
native costume in the basements of churches at home
hypnotized the faithful into contributing to an institution for which the term " futile " is far too
kind. As every child of the Rev. and Mrs. Luke
Hacket received from the board a salary of its own,
the worthy couple had not been idle, and in addition to this simple method of swelling their rev-
enue, the good man did a tidy little business in
vanilla—buying that fragrant bean at much less
than its market value from the poor and ignorant
Indians to whom he distributed tracts they could
not read. Whenever another little Hacket arrived,
he told the board, but the incredibly gullible body
knew nothing of his interest in the vanilla market.
As I was a stranger—he took me in. That is to
say, he wished me a happy new year and " touched "

me for five dollars—to go toward the purchase of a new organ for his Sunday school. I and my money were soon parted. Only afterwards did my hostess have a chance to tell me that among the colony the new organ was an old joke—that for many years tourists and visitors had contributed to its sweeter and, as yet, unheard melodies.

What was it? What is it? No one believed in his creed nor had the slightest interest in it. What lingering, reminiscent, perhaps in some instances atavistic misgiving and yearning to reverence, prompted these ill-assorted exiles to treat with a certain deference a person whom they really laughed at? There was an unsuspected pathos in it—the pathos of a world that involuntarily clutches at the straw it knows to be but yet a straw—the pathos of the exile who for the moment suffers even the distasteful if it in some way bridges the gulf between him and home. It was not politeness that restrained Mrs. Hammerton from smoking until the Hackets at last departed and that had caused our hostess, when she saw them coming, to discuss seriously with her husband whether or no she should temporarily banish the eggnog. What was it?

Mrs. Blythe, a slight, pretty woman prettily dressed had come in from her husband's ranch the week before for the holidays. In matter-of-fact tones she as giving her news to Mrs. Garvin, whose son was in charge of the town's electric light plant.

"As a rule one doesn't particularly mind calentura" (chills and fever), Mrs. Blythe was saying, "although it always leaves me rather weak. But what was so annoying this time, was the fact that Jack and I both had it at once and there wasn't anybody to take care of us. Delfina, the cook, chose that moment, of all moments, to get bitten in the calf of her leg by a snake. Horrid woman, Delfina —I'm sure she did it on purpose. Of course she was much worse than useless, for I had to take care of *her*—dose her with ammonia and cut live chickens in two and bind them on the place. You know—the hundred and fifty things one *always* does when they get bitten by snakes. If Joaquin the mayordomo had been around, I shouldn't have cared. He knows how to cook in a sort of way, and then, besides, I shouldn't have been so worried about the coffee picking. But poor Joaquin was in jail for stabbing his wife—yes, she died—and the jefe wouldn't let him out although I sent in a note saying how much we needed him for the next few weeks. It was deliberately disobliging of the jefe because we've had him to dinner several times and afterwards Jack always played cards with him and let him cheat. My temperature didn't go above a hundred and two and a half, but Jack's was a hundred and five off and on for three or four days, and when you pass the hundred mark, two and a half degrees make a great deal of difference. He was delirious a lot of the time and of course I couldn't let him fuss about the kitchen stove. The worst part was having to crawl out of bed and drag over to the tanks every afternoon to measure the coffee when the pickers came in. With Joaquin gone, there was nobody left who could read the lists and record the amounts. Then just as the quinine gave out, the river rose and no one could go to the village for more. Coming at that time of year, it was all really very annoying," she declared lightly and passed on to something else.

"Yes, that was how I caught this bad cold," another woman—whose husband manufactured coffee sacks—was explaining to some one. " There was the worst kind of a norther that night; I would have been soaked to the skin even if I hadn't slipped on a stone in the dark and fallen into the brook, and when I finally reached their hut I forgot the condition I was in. The poor little thing—she was only four—was absolutely rigid and having convulsion after convulsion. Her screams were frightful—it was impossible to control her—to get her to tell what the matter was, and nobody knew what had happened. She had simply given a shriek of terror and gone into convulsions. There was nothing to do—but nothing—*nothing*. At the end of an hour and a half she gave a final shriek and died, and when her poor little clenched fists relaxed, we found in one of them a dead scorpion. By that time I had begun to be very chilly and of course it ended in a bad cold. Two lumps please and no milk."

A servant in a starched skirt of watermelon pink and a starched white upper garment like a dressing sack glided out to help with the tea and cakes. A blue rebozo was draped about her neck and shoulders, her black hair hung to within a foot and a half of the floor in two fat braids, and in it, behind her right ear, was a pink camelia the color of her skirt. Her bare feet were thrust into slippers without heels or backs and as she slipped about from chair to chair they made a slight dragging sound on the tiles. Everyone said good afternoon to her as she handed the teacups, at which she smiled and replied in a respectful fashion that was, however, perfectly self-possessed.

"Did you hear about those people named Jackson who were here for a few days last month?" Mrs. Belding asked of the party in general. "You know they ended up at Cuernavaca and took a furnished house there meaning to stay all winter. Well, they stayed five days and then left—furious at Mexico and everyone in it." And she went on with considerable art and humor to sketch the brief career of the Jacksons. While they were at the hotel, before they took possession of their house, she told us, Mrs. Jackson had engaged servants—a mozo, two maids and a cook. The cook she stole from the Dressers. It wasn't at all nice of her to steal the cook as Mrs. Dresser had gone through a lot of bother for her about the renting of the house and had helped her to get the other servants. But Mrs. Jackson offered the creature two dollars more a month, and although she had lived at the Dressers for six years, she deserted them with a low, glad cry. Poor Mrs. Dresser rushed over to the Moons and sobbed when she told about it.

"Don't you worry, dear," said Mrs. Moon. "Leave that Jackson viper to me; I'll fix her. They move in this afternoon—I'm going up there to tea—and I promise you that you'll have your wall-eyed old dish-smasher hovering over the brasero in your kitchen by noon to-morrow."

Apparently Mrs. Moon did go to the Jacksons for tea and made herself most agreeable. " You may not believe it, but she really can once in a while," Mrs. Belding interjected. And as Mrs. Jackson had been conducting a Mexican establishment for about two hours, Mrs. Moon gave her all kinds of advice on the way to get along with the servants, ending with: " Of course you must *never* let the maids go out after dark even with their mothers, and it's *fatal* to give them breakfast. We simply don't do it in Mexico—not so much as a drop of coffee until noon. Breakfast always makes Mexicans insolent." Then Mrs. Moon, feeling that she was perhaps overdoing it, left while she saw that Mrs. Jackson was drinking it in in great, death-dealing gulps.

It was bad enough that night, Mrs. Belding ran on, when the cook and one of the maids tried to go to the serenata in the plaza. On the strength of the extra two dollars the cook had bought a new rebozo and wanted to wear it, and as there was no reason on earth why they shouldn't go to the serenata, they were mystified and angry at Mrs. Jackson's serenely declaring " No, no," and locking them in.

But the great seal of the Jacksons' fate was definitely affixed the next morning when Mrs. Jackson, up bright and early, with kind firmness, refused to let them make their coffee. Half an hour later Mrs. Moon experienced the bliss of seeing the mozo, the cook and the two maids wandering past her house— all weeping bitterly. Long before midday the cook was back at the Dressers; and from that moment Mrs. Jackson was blacklisted.

For five days she struggled to engage new servants, but she was believed to be a woman with a "bad heart." No one would go to her. She surrendered and left.

I did not altogether believe this tale of Mrs. Belding's, nor did I believe the man who casually told us that a few weeks before, the authorities had, just in time, interrupted a human sacrifice in an Indian village some twenty or thirty miles up from the coast. After nearly four hundred years of Christianity the Indians had, it seemed, dug up a large stone idol and attempted to revert. Then, too, the remark of a young girl who had been visiting in Vera Cruz struck me as rather incredible. "I was there for a month," she said. "Yes, there was some yellow fever and a great deal of smallpox—but when you're having a good time, who minds smallpox?"

It was all so new to me in matter and manner, so sprinkled with easy references to objects, scenes, and conditions I had met with only in highfalutin stories lacking the ring of truth, so ornate with "meandering" (thank you, Robert Browning), Spanish words whose meaning I did not know. There was also among the men much coffee talk—a whole new world to one who has always taken for granted that coffee originates, roasted, ground and done up in five-pound tins on a grocer's shelves. But it was all true even to the interrupted human sacrifice and the fact that some of the shrubs among the roses and heliotrope near the piazza were coffee trees. Had I never seen the little colony again I should always have remembered it as a picturesque, romantic and delightful thing. And how—I told myself as I sat there listening and looking—they must, away off here, depend upon one another for society, both in a formal and in an intimate sense! How they must come together and somewhat wistfully try to forget Mexico in talking of home in their own language! What it is, after all, to understand and be understood!—and all that sort of thing. If my first afternoon with foreigners in Mexico had been my last, I should have carried away with me a brave, bright colored little picture of much charm and some pathos. However, since then I have spent with my compatriots in this interesting land days innumerable.

I fear I am, for the delightful purposes of art, unfortunately unselective. First impressions have their value; they have, indeed, very great value, and of a kind quite their own. As my first impression of Americans in Mexico was the kind I have just been trying to give, and as it was to me wholly interesting and more agreeable than not, I ought, perhaps, to let it stand; but somehow I can't. My inartistic impulse to keep on and tell all the little I know, instead of stopping at the right place, is too strong.

There are said to be about thirty thousand American residents in the Mexican Republic, and the men pursue vocations ranging from that of tramp to that of president of great and successful business ventures. There are American doctors and dentists, brakemen, locomotive engineers, Pullman-car conductors, civil engineers, mining engineers, " promoters," grocers, hotel keepers, dealers in curios; there are American barkeepers, lawyers, stenographers, photographers, artists, clerks, electricians, and owners of ranches of one kind or another who grow cattle or coffee or vanilla or sugar or rubber.

Many Americans are managers of some sort—they manage mines or plantations or railways, or the local interests of some manufacturing or business concern in the United States. One meets Americans—both men and women—on the streets, in hotels, in shops, strolling or sitting in the plaza—almost everywhere in the course of the day's work, and in the course of the day's play, one may drop in at the house of some acquaintance or friend and have a cup of tea, with the usual accompaniments, at four or half past. I am speaking now not of the City of Mexico, whose American colony as a colony I know solely through the " Society " notes of the *Mexican Herald*. From that authentic source he who runs may read (or he who reads may run) that on almost any afternoon at the large entertainment given by Mrs. Brooks for her popular friend, Mrs. Crooks, punch was served at a refreshment table quaintly decorated with smilax by the ever-charming Mrs. Snooks. That there are agreeable Americans living in the city I am sure, because I have met some of them elsewhere. But of American society in general there I am only competent to suspect that, like society in most places, it is considerably less important and entrancing in reality than it is in print.

VIVA MEXICO!

In the smaller places, even when there are residents of the United States in numbers sufficiently great to be regarded as a " colony," there is absolutely nothing that by any stretch of imagination or spread of printer's ink could be called " American society." The New Year's Day I have mentioned seems to me now a kind of freak of nature; I am at a loss to account for it. For since then my knowledge of Americans in the small towns has become considerable, and they are not in the least as I supposed they were. They do *not* depend upon one another; they do not come together to talk wistfully of home in the mother tongue; they do *not* understand one another, and by one another they are *not* understood! There is at best about most of their exceedingly few relations an atmosphere of petty and ungenerous gossip, and at worst a fog— a positive sand storm of enmity and hatred through which it takes a really ludicrous amount of delicate navigation successfully to steer oneself. As a body they simply do not meet. There are, instead, groups of two, of three, of four, who have tea together (other forms of entertainment are rarely attempted) chiefly for the purpose of envitrioling the others. There are among them agreeable groups and truly charming individuals, but when they allow themselves to assimilate at all, it is usually in a most reluctant, acid, and malnutritious form (a singularly repulsive figure of speech, come to think of it) that does no one any good. It is not unamusing just at first to have a lady inform you with tremulous lips and in a tense, white voice that if you call on Mrs. X., you must not expect to call any longer on *her*; and I confess I have enjoyed learning in great detail just why this one is no longer speaking to that, and the train of events that led up to Mr. A.'s finally slapping the face of Mr. B. Yet there are well-defined limits to intellectual treats of this nature, and one quickly longs for entertainment at once less dramatic and more varied.

Among the Americans this is difficult to get, although, as I pause and recall with gratitude and affection some of my friends in Jalapa, for instance, I am tempted to retract this statement. The trouble lies, I feel sure, in the fact that, having come from widely dissimilar parts of the United States, and having had while there affiliations, in many instances, whose slight difference is still great enough to make a great difference, they have but little in common. And Mexican towns are utterly lacking in those diverse interests that at home supply the women of even very small communities with so many pleasant and harmless, if artificial, bonds. The Mexican theater is crude and impossible—even if the fractious ladies knew Spanish sufficiently well to follow rapid dialogue with enjoyment, which they rarely do. The occasional traveling opera company, with one wind-busted, middle-aged star who twenty-five years ago was rumored to have been well received in Rio de Janeiro, is a torture; there are no notable piano or song recitals, no King's Daughters or other pet charities, no D. A. R.'s, no one to interpret the "Ring and the Book," or the "Ring of the Niebelungen," no one to give chafing-dish lectures or inspire enthusiasm for things like the etchings of Whistler and the economical cremation of garbage, the abolishment of child labor, and the encouragement of the backyard beautiful. Beyond the slight and monotonous cares of housekeeping on a small scale, there is little to occupy their time; there are, in a word, no varied outlets available for their normal socio-intellectual energies, and of course the distressing happens. Even the one or two common bonds they might have, most unfortunately act not as bonds at all. The "servant problem," for instance, small as wages are, serves only to keep them farther apart, and apparently friendship between two families engaged in the same kind of enterprise is almost impossible. Very rarely have I seen two coffee-growers who were not virulently jealous of each other's successes, and who would not, in a business way, cut each other's throats without a qualm if by doing so they could come out a few dollars ahead.

Indeed, from the little I have seen and the great deal I have heard of my countrymen's business coups in Mexico, I cannot believe that transplantation has a tendency to elevate one's ethics. It is, perhaps, unnecessary to record that I know men in Mexico whose methods of business are fastidiously honorable with Mexican and compatriot alike, but they are extremely rare; far more rare than they are at home. If in Mexico I were forced to choose between trusting in a business matter to the representations of a Mexican whom I knew and liked and an American whom I knew and liked, I should, except in one or two cases, where I should be betting, so to speak, on a certainty, trust the Mexican.

An always interesting phase of the American in Mexico is the annual invasion of the country, from January to March, by immense parties of " personally conducted " tourists from the United States.

VIVA MEXICO!

In private cars—even in private trains—they descend every few days upon the cities and towns of chief pictorial and historic interest, and just as the American residents of England, Germany, Italy, and France shudder at the ancient and honorable name of " Thomas Cook and Sons," do the Americans who have chosen Mexico as the land of their adoption shrug and laugh at the mention of " las turistas." On general principles, to shrug and sneer—for in this laugh there always lurks a sneer —merely because a hundred and fifty amiable creatures have chosen to be herded from one end of a vast foreign country and back again in two weeks, would seem to be narrow and pointless. But I have grown to consider it, for principles quite specific, neither the one nor the other. The American resident's sneer is unfortunately a helpless, ineffectual one, but he is without question sometimes entitled to it.

Somebody once wrote an article—perhaps it was a whole book—which he called " The Psychology of Crowds." I did not read it, but many years ago, when it came out, the title imbedded itself in my mind as a wonderfully suggestive title that didn't suggest to me anything at all. Since then I have had frequent occasion to excavate it, and without having read a word of the work, I am convinced that I know exactly what the author meant. Did he, I often wonder, ever study, in his study of crowds, a crowd of American tourists in Mexico? What a misfortune for his book if he neglected to! They are, it seems, composed of the most estimable units of which one can conceive; the sort of persons who make a "world's fair" possible; the salt of the earth—"the backbone of the nation." And yet when they unite and start out on their travels, a kind of madness now and then seizes upon them; not continuously, and sometimes not at all, but now and then. Young girls who, at home, could be trusted on every occasion to conduct themselves with a kind of provincial dignity; sensible, middle-aged fathers and mothers of grown-up families, and old women with white water-waves and gray lisle-thread gloves, will now and then, when on a tour in Mexico, go out of their way to do things that make the very peons blush. The great majority of tourists are, of course, quiet, well-behaved persons who take an intelligent interest in their travels. It is to the exception I am referring; the exception by whom the others, alas! are judged.

The least of their crimes is their suddenly ac-

quired mania for being conspicuous. At home, in
their city side streets, their humdrum suburbs, their
placid villages, they have been content for thirty,
fifty, seventy years to pursue their various decent
ways, legitimately observed and clad appropriately
to their means and station. But once arrived in the
ancient capital of Montezuma, many of them are
inspired in the most astounding fashion to attract
attention to themselves. On Sunday afternoon, in
the crowded Paseo, I have seen, for instance, in
cabs, undoubtedly respectable women from my
country with enormous straw sombreros on their
heads, and about their shoulders those brilliant and
hideous " Mexican " sarapes—woven for the tourist trade, it is said, in Germany. All the rest of
the world was, of course, in its Paris best, and
staring at them with amazed eyes. In Mexico the
only possible circumstance under which a native
woman of any position whatever would wear a peon
hat would be a hot day in the depths of the country,
were she forced to travel in an open vehicle or on
horseback. As for sarapes, they, of course, are
worn only by men. The effect these travelers produced upon the local mind was somewhat analo-
gous to that which a party of Mexican ladies would
produce upon the mind of New York should they

decide to drive up Fifth Avenue wearing policemen's helmets and variegated trousers. Only Mexican women would never do the one, while American women frequently, from motives I am at a loss
to account for, do the other.

Then, once in a small town to which large parties rarely go, I saw half a dozen men and women
suddenly detach themselves from their crowd on
being told that a certain middle-aged man, bidding
good-by to some guests at his front door, was the
governor of the state. At a distance of from ten
to fifteen feet of him they deliberately focused
their kodaks on the group and pressed the button.
Afterwards I asked one of the men with whom
the governor had been talking, if the governor had
commented upon the matter. " Why, yes," was the
reply. " He said, with a shrug, ' Obviously from
the United States,' and then went on with his conversation."

At Tehuacan, one winter, the women in a party
of between twenty and thirty, quite innocently (although most commonly) left behind them an odious
impression that the few resident Americans who
happened to be staying at the place were powerless
to eradicate. The man in charge of them could not
speak Spanish, and had with him an interpreter, a

Mexican boy of seventeen or eighteen who knew
a moderate amount of English. He was a pretty-
eyed, clever-looking little person, and the women
of the party had come to treat him much as one
might treat a pet animal of docile habits. They
would stroke and ruffle his shock of black hair,
pinch his cheeks, " hold hands " with him when
walking through the long corridors, adjust his red
cravat if it wasn't straight, and coquettishly struggle with one another for the privilege of strolling
with him in the garden. To me it meant no more
than a disagreeably playful exhibition of bad taste,
but the Mexicans in the hotel regarded a young
man of eighteen, in his station of life, as being of
a marriageable age, which, of course, he was, and
they could not be made to see in the situation anything but that the American women were in love
with him and unable to conceal it in public. Some
of them with young daughters talked of appealing
to the hotel proprietor to eject persons of this description. In the United States a party of Mexican
women would under no circumstances hold hands
with, say, a bellboy, or stroke the hair of a waiter.

In Puebla it is told that some American tourists
ate their luncheon in the cathedral, threw orange
peel and sardine tins on the floor, and upon leaving

washed their hands in the holy water. I don't vouch for this story; I merely believe it. And by reason of such things and a hundred others, the American resident is entitled to his sneer. For he himself, in at least his relations with the natives, is accustomed to display something of their courtesy, their dignity. He resents not only the unfortunate and lasting impression many of his compatriots leave upon the populace, but its disastrous effect upon the populace itself. When American tourists, armed with penknives, cut out squares of Gobelin tapestry from the furniture of the President's drawing-room, it is always a simple matter for the President to close Chapultepec to the public; but when they encourage "humorous" familiarities with well-mannered, unsophisticated servants and the lower classes generally, there is no remedy. Chiefly from constant contact with tourists, the cab drivers of the City of Mexico have become notoriously extortionate and insolent, and, for the same reason, Cuernavaca, one of the most beautiful little towns, not only in Mexico, but in the world, may soon—tourist-ridden as it is—be one of the least attractive. There, among the cabmen, the hotel employees, the guides, and the mozos who have horses for hire, the admirable native manner has lamentably deteriorated. Egged on by underbred Americans, many of them have themselves become common, impudent, and a bore. They no longer suggest Mexico. One might almost as well " see Naples and die."

XIII

WHEN my first New Year's party dispersed, I walked back to the center of the town with a man who had lived for many years in Mexico, who had been everywhere and had done everything, and who seemed to know something funny or tragic or scandalous about everybody in the world. He loved to talk, to describe, to recall; and while we had some drinks together at a café under the sky-blue portales, he aroused my interest in people I never had heard of and never should see. He told me, among other things, about the Trawnbeighs.

This, as nearly as I can remember, is what he told me about the Trawnbeighs:

The Trawnbeighs, he said, were the sort of people who " dressed for dinner," even when, as sometimes happened, they had no dinner in the house to dress for. It is perhaps unnecessary to add that the Trawnbeighs were English. Indeed, on looking back, I often feel that to my first apparently flippant statement it is unnecessary to add *anything*.

230

For to one who knew Mr. and Mrs. Trawnbeigh, Edwina, Violet, Maud, and Cyril, it was the first and last word on them; their alpha and omega, together with all that went between. Not that the statement *is* flippant—far from it. There is in it a seriousness, a profundity, an immense philosophic import. At times it has almost moved me to lift my hat, very much as one does for reasons of state, or religion, or death.

This, let me hasten to explain, is not at all the way I feel when I put on evening clothes myself, which I do at least twice out of my every three hundred and sixty-five opportunities. No born American could feel that way about his own dress coat. He sometimes thinks he does; he often—and isn't it boresome!—pretends he does, but he really doesn't. As a matter of unimportant fact, the born American may have " dressed " every evening of his grown-up life. But if he found himself on an isolated, played-out Mexican coffee and vanilla finca, with a wife, four children, a tiled roof that leaked whenever there was a " norther," an unsealed sala through the bamboo partitions of which a cold, wet wind howled sometimes for a week at a time, with no money, no capacity for making any, no " prospects " and no cook—under these depressing circumstances it is impossible to conceive of an American dressing for dinner every night at a quarter before seven in any spirit but one of ghastly humor.

With the Trawnbeighs' performance of this sacred rite, however, irony and humor had nothing to do. The Trawnbeighs had a robust sense of fun (so, I feel sure, have pumpkins and turnips and the larger varieties of the nutritious potato family); but humor, when they didn't recognize it, bewildered them, and it always struck them as just a trifle underbred when they did.

Trawnbeigh had come over to Mexico—" come out from England," he would have expressed it—as a kind of secretary to his cousin, Sir Somebody Something, who was building a harbor or a railway or a canal (I don't believe Trawnbeigh himself ever knew just what it was) for a British company down in the hot country. Mrs. Trawnbeigh, with her young, was to follow on the next steamer a month later; and as she was in mid-ocean when Sir Somebody suddenly died of yellow fever, she did not learn of this inopportune event until it was too late to turn back. Still I doubt whether she would have turned back if she could. For, as Trawnbeigh once explained to me, at a time when they literally hadn't enough to eat (a hail storm had not only destroyed his coffee crop, but had frozen the roots of most of his trees, and the price of vanilla had fallen from ten cents a bean to three and a half), leaving England at all, he explained, had necessitated "burning their bridges behind them." He did not tell me the nature of their bridges, nor whether they had made much of a blaze. In fact, that one vague, inflammatory allusion was the nearest approach to a personal confidence Trawnbeigh was ever known to make in all his fifteen years of Mexican life.

The situation, when he met Mrs. Trawnbeigh and the children on the dock at Vera Cruz, was extremely dreary, and at the end of a month it had grown much worse, although the Trawnbeighs apparently didn't think so. They even spoke and wrote as if their affairs were " looking up a bit." For, after a few weeks of visiting among kindly compatriots at Vera Cruz and Rebozo, Mrs. Trawnbeigh became cook for some English engineers (there were seven of them) in a sizzling, mosquitoey, feverish mudhole on the Isthmus of Tehuantepec. The Trawnbeighs didn't call it " cook," neither did the seven engineers. I don't believe the engineers even thought of it as cook. (What Mrs. Trawnbeigh thought of it will never

be known.) How *could* they when that lady, after
feeding the four little Trawnbeighs (or rather the
four young Trawnbeighs; they had never been
little) a meal I think they called " the nursery
tea," managed every afternoon, within the next two
hours, first to create out of nothing a perfectly
edible dinner for nine persons, and, secondly, to
receive them all at seven forty-five in a red-striped,
lemon satin ball gown (it looked like poisonous
wall paper), eleven silver bangles, a cameo necklace, and an ostrich tip sprouting from the top
of her head. Trawnbeigh, too, was in evening
clothes. And they didn't call it cooking; they
spoke of it as " looking after the mess " or " keeping an eye on the young chaps' livers." Nevertheless, Mrs. Trawnbeigh, daughter of the late the
Honorable Cyril Cosby Godolphin Dundas and the
late Clare Walpurga Emmeline Moate, cooked—
and cooked hard—for almost a year; at the end of
which time she was stricken with what she was
pleased to refer to as " a bad go of fevah."

Fortunately, they were spared having to pass
around the hat, although it would have amounted
to that if Trawnbeigh hadn't, after the pleasant
English fashion, come into some money. In the
United States people know to a cent what they may

expect to inherit, and then they sometimes don't get it; but in England there seems to be an endless succession of retired and unmarried army officers who die every little while in Jermyn Street and leave two thousand pounds to a distant relative they have never met. Something like this happened to Trawnbeigh, and on the prospect of his legacy he was able to pull out of the Tehuantepec mud-hole and restore his wife to her usual state of health in the pure and bracing air of Rebozo.

Various things can be done with two thousand pounds, but just what *shall* be done ought to depend very largely on whether they happen to be one's first two thousand or one's last. Trawnbeigh, however, invested his ("interred" would be a more accurate term) quite as if they never would be missed. The disposition to be a country gentleman was in Trawnbeigh's blood. Indeed, the first impression one received from the family was that everything they did was in their blood. It never seemed to me that Trawnbeigh had immediately sunk the whole of his little fortune in an old, small, and dilapidated coffee place so much because he was dazzled by the glittering financial future the shameless owner (another Englishman, by the way) predicted for him, as because to own an estate and live on it was, so to speak, his natural element. He had tried, while Mrs. Trawnbeigh was cooking on the Isthmus, to get " something to do." But there was really nothing in Mexico he *could* do. He was splendidly strong, and in the United States he very cheerfully, and with no loss of self-respect or point of view, would have temporarily shoveled wheat or coal, or driven a team, or worked on the street force, as many another Englishman of noble lineage has done before and since; but in the tropics an Anglo-Saxon cannot be a day laborer. He can't because he can't. And there was in Mexico no clerical position open to Trawnbeigh because he did not know Spanish. (It is significant that after fifteen consecutive years of residence in the country, *none* of the Trawnbeighs knew Spanish.) To be, somehow and somewhere, an English country gentleman of a well-known, slightly old-fashioned type, was as much Trawnbeigh's destiny as it is the destiny of, say, a polar bear to be a polar bear or a camel to be a camel. As soon as he got his two thousand pounds he became one.

When I first met them all he had been one for about ten years. I had recently settled in Trawnbeigh's neighborhood, which in Mexico means that my ranch was a hard day-and-a-half ride from his, over roads that are not roads, but merely ditches full of liquefied mud on the level stretches, and ditches full of assorted boulders on the ascent. So, although we looked neighborly on a small map, I might not have had the joy of meeting the Trawnbeighs for years if my mule hadn't gone lame one day when I was making the interminable trip to Rebozo. Trawnbeigh's place was seven miles from the main road, and as I happened to be near the parting of the ways when the off hind leg of Catalina began to limp, I decided to leave her with my mozo at an Indian village until a pack train should pass by (there is always some one in a pack train who can remove a bad shoe), while I proceeded on the mozo's mule to the Trawnbeighs'. My usual stopping place for the night was five miles farther on, and the Indian village was—well, it was an Indian village. Time and again I had been told of Trawnbeigh's early adventures, and I felt sure he could "put me up" (as he would have said himself) for the night. He "put me up" not only that night, but as my mozo didn't appear until late the next afternoon, a second night as well. And when I at last rode away, it was with the feeling of having learned from the Trawnbeighs a great lesson.

In the first place they couldn't have expected me; they couldn't possibly have expected anyone. And it was a hot afternoon. But as it was the hour at which people at " home " dropped in for tea, Mrs. Trawnbeigh and her three plain, heavy looking daughters were perfectly prepared to dispense hospitality to any number of mythical friends. They had on hideous but distinctly " dressy " dresses of amazingly stamped materials known, I believe, as " summer silks," and they were all four tightly laced. Current fashion in Paris, London, and New York by no means insisted on small, smooth, round waists, but the Trawnbeigh women had them because (as it gradually dawned on me) to have had any other kind would have been a concession to anatomy and the weather. To anything so compressible as one's anatomy, or as vulgarly impartial as the weather, the Trawnbeighs simply did not concede. I never could get over the feeling that they all secretly regarded weather in general as a kind of popular institution, of vital importance only to the middle class. Cyril, an extremely beautiful young person of twenty-two, who had been playing tennis (by himself) on the asoleadero, was in " flannels," and Trawnbeigh admirably looked the part in gray, middle-aged riding things, although, as I discovered before leaving, their stable at the time consisted of one senile burro with ingrowing hoofs.

From the first it all seemed too flawless to be true. I had never visited in England, but I doubt if there is another country whose literature gives one so definite and lasting an impression of its " home life." Perhaps this is because the life of families of the class to which the Trawnbeighs belonged proceeds in England by such a series of definite and traditional episodes. In a household like theirs, the unexpected must have a devil of a time in finding a chance to happen. For, during my visit, absolutely nothing happened that I hadn't long since chuckled over in making the acquaintance of Jane Austen, Thackeray, George Eliot, and Anthony Trollope; not to mention Ouida (it was Cyril, of course, who from time to time struck the Ouida note), and the more laborious performances of Mrs. Humphrey Ward. They all of them did at every tick of the clock precisely what they ought to have done. They were a page, the least bit crumpled, torn from " Half Hours with the Best Authors," and cast, dear Heaven! upon a hillside in darkest Mexico.

Of course we had tea in the garden. There wasn't any garden, but we nevertheless had tea in it. The house would have been cooler, less glaring, and free from the venomous little rodadoras that stung the backs of my hands full of microscopic polka dots; but we all strolled out to a spot some fifty yards away where a bench, half a dozen shaky, homemade chairs, and a rustic table were most imperfectly shaded by three tattered banana trees.

"We love to drink tea in the dingle dangle," Mrs. Trawnbeigh explained. How the tea tray itself got to the "dingle dangle," I have only a general suspicion, for when we arrived it was already there, equipped with caddy, cozy, a plate of buttered toast, a pot of strawberry jam, and all the rest of it. But try as I might, I simply could not rid myself of the feeling that at least two footmen had arranged it all and then discreetly retired; a feeling that also sought to account for the tray's subsequent removal, which took place while Trawnbeigh, Cyril, Edwina, and I walked over to inspect the asoleadero and washing tanks. I wanted to look back; but something (the fear, perhaps, of being turned into a pillar of salt) restrained me.

With most English-speaking persons in that part of the world, conversation has to do with coffee, coffee and—coffee. The Trawnbeighs, however, scarcely touched on the insistent topic. While we sat on the low wall of the dilapidated little asoleadero we discussed pheasant shooting and the "best places" for haberdashery and "Gladstone bags." Cyril, as if it were but a matter of inclination, said he thought he might go over for the shooting that year; a cousin had asked him "to make a seventh." I never found out what this meant and didn't have the nerve to ask.

"Bertie shoots the twelfth, doesn't he?" Edwina here inquired.

To which her brother replied, as if she had shown a distressing ignorance of some fundamental date in history, like 1066 or 1215, "Bertie *always* shoots the twelfth."

The best place for haberdashery in Mr. Trawnbeigh's opinion was "the Stores." But Cyril preferred a small shop in Bond Street, maintaining firmly, but with good humor, that it was not merely, as "the pater" insisted, because the fellow charged more, but because one didn't "run the risk of seeing some beastly bounder in a cravat uncommonly like one's own." Trawnbeigh, as a sedate parent bordering on middle age, felt obliged to stand up for the more economical "Stores," but it was evident that he really admired Cyril's exclusive principles and approved of them. Edwina cut short the argument with an abrupt question.

" I say," she inquired anxiously, "has the dressing
bell gone yet?" The dressing bell hadn't gone, but
it soon went. For Mr. Trawnbeigh, after looking
at his watch, bustled off to the house and rang it
himself. Then we withdrew to our respective
apartments to dress for dinner.

" I've put you in the north wing, old man; there's
always a breeze in the wing," my host declared as
he ushered me into a bamboo shed they used apparently for storing corn and iron implements of
an agricultural nature. But there was also in the
room a recently made-up cot with real sheets, a tin
bath tub, hot and cold water in two earthenware
jars, and an empty packing case upholstered in oil-
cloth. When Trawnbeigh spoke of this last as a
" wash-hand-stand," I knew I had indeed strayed
from life into the realms of mid-Victorian romance.

The breeze Trawnbeigh had referred to developed
in the violent Mexican way, while I was enjoying
the bath tub, into an unmistakable norther. Water
fell on the roof like so much lead and then sprang
off (some of it did) in thick, round streams from the
tin spouts; the wind screamed in and out of the tiles
overhead, and through the " north wing's " blurred
windows the writhing banana trees of the " dingle
dangle " looked like strange things one sees in an

aquarium. As soon as I could get into my clothes
again—a bath was as far as I was able to live up to
the Trawnbeigh ideal—I went into the sala where
the dinner table was already set with a really heart-
rending attempt at splendor. I have said that nothing happened with which I had not a sort of literary
acquaintance; but I was wrong. While I was
standing there wondering how the Trawnbeighs
had been able all those years to keep it up, a window in the next room blew open with a bang. I
ran in to shut it; but before I reached it, I stopped
short and, as hastily and quietly as I could, tiptoed
back to the " wing." For the next room was the
kitchen and at one end of it Trawnbeigh, in a
shabby but perfectly fitting dress-coat, his trousers
rolled up halfway to his knees, was patiently holding an umbrella over his wife's sacred dinner gown,
while she—bebangled, becameoed, beplumed, and
stripped to the buff—masterfully cooked our dinner
on the brasero.

To me it was all extremely wonderful, and the
wonder of it did not lessen during the five years in
which, on my way to and from Rebozo, I stopped
over at the Trawnbeighs' several times a year. For,
although I knew that they were often financially all
but down and out, the endless red tape of their daily

life never struck me as being merely a pathetic bluff. Their rising bells and dressing bells, their apparent dependence on all sorts of pleasant accessories that simply did not exist, their occupations (I mean those on which I did not have to turn a tactful back, such as " botanizing," " crewel work," painting horrible water colors and composing long lists of British-sounding things to be " sent out from the Stores "), the informality with which we waited on ourselves at luncheon and the stately, punctilious manner in which we did precisely the same thing at dinner, the preordained hour at which Mrs. Trawnbeigh and the girls each took a candle and said good night, leaving Trawnbeigh, Cyril, and me to smoke a pipe and " do a whisky peg " (Trawnbeigh had spent some years in India), the whole inflexibly insular scheme of their existence was more, infinitely more, than a bluff. It was a placid, tenacious clinging to the straw of their ideal in a great, deep sea of poverty, discomfort, and isolation. And it had its reward.

For after fourteen years of Mexican life, Cyril was almost exactly what he would have been had he never seen the place; and Cyril was the Trawnbeigh's one asset of immense value. He was most agreeable to look at, he was both related to and con-

nected with many of the most historical-sounding
ladies and gentlemen in England, and he had just
the limited, selfish, amiable outlook on the world in
general that was sure (granting the other things)
to impress Miss Irene Slapp of Pittsburg as the
height of both breeding and distinction.

Irene Slapp had beauty and distinction of her own.
Somehow, although they all "needed the money,"
I don't believe Cyril would have married her if she
hadn't. Anyhow, one evening in the City of Mexico
he took her in to dinner at the British Legation
where he had been asked to dine as a matter of
course, and before the second entrée, Miss Slapp was
slightly in love with him and very deeply in love
with the scheme of life, the standard, the ideal, or
whatever you choose to call it, he had inherited and
had been brought up, under staggering difficulties,
to represent.

"The young beggar has made a pot of money in
the States," Trawnbeigh gravely informed me after
Cyril had spent seven weeks in Pittsburg—whither
he had been persuaded to journey on the Slapp's
private train.

"And, you know I've decided to sell the old
place," he casually remarked a month or so later.
"Yes, yes," he went on, "the young people are be-

ginning to leave us." (I hadn't noticed any signs of impending flight on the part of Edwina, Violet, and Maud.) " Mrs. Trawnbeigh and I want to end our days at home. Slapp believes there's gold on the place—or would it be petroleum? He's welcome to it. After all, I've never been fearfully keen on business."

And I rode away pondering, as I always did, on the great lesson of the Trawnbeighs.

XIV

EARLY in the eighteenth century there went to Mexico from France a boy of sixteen named Joseph de la Borde. " By his fortunate mining ventures at Tlalpujahua, Tasco, and Zacatecas," we read, " he made a fortune of forty million pesos." One of these millions he spent in building a church at Tasco, and another he spent in building a garden at Cuernavaca. This is all I know about Joseph de la Borde, or, as he was called in Mexico, José de la Borda, except that he died in Cuernavaca at the age of seventy-nine and that his portrait—a funny old man in a white wig and black velvet—hangs among the portraits of other dead and eminent gentlemen in an obscure corridor of the National Museum. It might be interesting to learn what became of the remaining thirty-eight millions; but then again it might not. So I haven't tried to find out. It is scarcely probable, however, that at a later date he expressed himself more notably than he did in the construction of El Jardin Borda.

It lies on a steep hillside behind Cuernavaca, and

even if it were not one of the most beautiful of
tangled, neglected, ruined old gardens anywhere, it
would be lovable for the manner in which it tried
so hard to be a French garden and failed. Joseph,
it is clear, had the French passion for formalizing
the landscape—for putting Nature into a pretty
strait-jacket; but although he spent much time and
a million pesos in trying to do this at Cuernavaca,
he rather wonderfully did not succeed. No doubt
the result pleased him; it surely ought to have. But
just as surely it was not the light, bright, definitely
graceful result of which his French mind had conceived. It was always a little precious to speak of
one thing in terms of another, but nevertheless there
is about a perfect French garden something very
musical. The Luxembourg garden is musical, so is
the garden at Versailles; musical with the kind of
music that is as deliberately academic as it is deliberately tuneful. There was every endeavor to
make the Jardin Borda perform on a small scale
with the same blithe elegance of Versailles and the
garden of the Luxembourg; but it was Mexican at
heart. Perhaps it foresaw Napoleon III. At any
rate, although it tried to be French, it at the last
refused.

The situation, the flora, and, absurd as it may

sound, the technic of the stone masons who built
the architectural features—the walls, the fountains,
the summerhouses, the cascades, and the ponds—all
combine to give the place an individuality, sometimes
Spanish, sometimes Mexican, but French only in the
same remote manner in which Shakespeare is Shakespeare when Madame Bernhardt, instead of exclaiming, "Go. Stand not upon the order of your going,
but go at once," liquidly burbles: "Allez, messieurs;
allez immédiatement—sans cérémonie!" It hangs
precipitously on the side of a ravine when it should
have been level (one is so glad it is not), and the
dense, southern trees—mangoes and sapotes and
Indian laurel—with which it was planted, have long
since outgrown the scale of the place, interlaced and
roofed out the sky overhead with an opaque and
somber canopy. They now are not, as they were intended to be, decorative features of the garden, they
are the garden itself; one cannot see the trees for
the forest. In its impermeable shade there are long,
islanded tanks in which many numerous families of
ducks and geese live a strangely secluded, dignified,
aristocratic existence—arbors of roses and jasmine,
and heavy, broken old fountains that no longer play
and splash. In fact, all the masonry, and to retain
itself on the hillside the place had to be a mass

249

of masonry, is heavy and simple, and except for the arbors there are no longer any flowers. Where in the days of Joseph there no doubt used to be a dazzling carpet of color, there is now only a tangle of coffee trees. But in Cuernavaca when the purple and red and pink of growing things under a pitiless sun become intolerable, the absence of color in the Jardin Borda, except for its dark and soothing green, is well worth frequently paying the twenty-five centavos the present owner charges as an admittance fee.

In seventy-five or a hundred years there will be many fine old formal gardens in the United States—finer than the Borda ever was. Under the pergolas of some of them there is much tea and pleasant conversation and one greatly admires their marble furniture imported from Italy—their careful riot of flowers. But at present it is difficult to forget that their prevailing color is wealth, and to forget it will take at least another century. If they have everything that Joseph's garden lacks, they all lack the thing it has. For in its twilit arbors and all along its sad and silent terraces there is at any hour the same poetic mystery that even at the ages of eight and four sometimes used to affect Don Guillermo and me when we were turned loose to play and to pick daisies in the Borghese garden in Rome. The Borghese is extensive and the Borda is tiny, but history has strolled in both of them and they both seem to have beautiful, secret sorrows.

I am not like an American woman tourist in Cuernavaca (it was her first week in the country) who informed me that she sat in the hotel all day because she was so tired of seeing the streets full of Mexicans! "You know, we saw a great many Mexicans in Mexico City," she added in the aggrieved tone of one who thinks it is high time for a procession of Swedes or Australians. But in Mexico, as elsewhere, there are mornings and afternoons when it is good to be out of range of the human voice and alone with trees, a sheet of water however small, and some animals.

Attached to the grounds is a house—a succession of cool rooms on one floor, and in passing the open doors and windows of the long, denuded sala as one begins to descend the main terrace, it is impossible not to remember for a moment that the place was lived in by Maximilian and Carlotta. It is impossible, too, especially if the white roses and jasmine of the arbor are in bloom, not to pay the unfortunate lady and gentleman the tribute of a sentimental pang. In Mexico one often finds oneself thinking

251

of Maximilian and Carlotta and, on the whole, with a kindliness springing, I am sure, chiefly from the facts that they were young and in love. For politically they were but a pair of stupid mistakes. History has been kind to Maximilian—far kinder than he deserved—but standard and respectable history is so timorous of leaving a wrong impression that it often fails to leave any impression at all. History to be interesting and valuable should be recorded by persons of talent and prejudice or by chambermaids who listen at keyholes.

As it is difficult to believe Maximilian a scoundrel, the other belief most open to one in view of his brief career, is that he was a dull, ignorant, and fatuous young man who thought it would prove more diverting to be a Mexican emperor than an Austrian archduke. His portrait, indeed (the famous one on horseback now in the National Palace), expresses just this with unconscious cruelty. History often speaks of him as handsome—an adjective that even the idealized portrait in question quite fails to justify. Without more chin than Maximilian ever had, one can be neither handsome nor a successful emperor. He was amiable and " well disposed," but his fatuity revealed itself from the first in the mere fact of his being able to see in himself a logical claimant to the throne of Mexico in the far-fetched and absurd reason that led Napoleon III and the Roman Catholic Church to select him. For he was chosen to adorn this precariously fictitious seat because Mexico had formerly been a Spanish possession and the house of which he was a representative had ruled in Spain before the accession of the Bourbons! Napoleon III naturally was not giving away empires to Bourbons, and Maximilian was supposed " to reunite the Mexico of 1863 with the monarchical Mexico of 1821." To the party of intelligence, progress, and reform there was about the same amount of right and reason in this as the inhabitants of France would find in a sudden demand on my part to be made their chief executive because my name happens to be a French name.

Maximilian " accepted " the crown on two conditions. That he was pathetically ignorant of at least the subject on which he ought to have been best informed is clear from one of them, and that he was dull becomes almost as evident from the other. The first provided that he should be elected to the throne of Mexico by popular vote; and the second, that the Emperor Napoleon should give him armed aid as long as he required it. Now anyone with the most rudimentary knowledge of Mexico knows that a

popular election there is an impossibility and always
has been. No one in Mexico is ever elected by popular vote, or ever really elected at all. It cannot be
done at the present time (1908) any more than it
could have been when Maximilian and Carlotta were
crowned in the cathedral in 1864. The inhabitants
of Mexico, incredible as it may sound, speak more
than fifty totally different languages and many of
them have never learned Spanish. Some of them in
fact—the Yaquis in Sonora and the Mayas in Yucatan—do not even recognize the Mexican Government, are still at war with it and are being for this
reason rapidly exterminated, although not as rapidly
as would be the case if the military exterminators
did not receive increased pay while engaged in the
congenial pursuit of extermination. When one con-
siders that two years before the proposed taking of
the census in 1910, the Government is planning a
gradual and elaborate campaign of enlightenment
in the hope of allaying the suspicions of the superstitious lower classes and making a more or less accurate census possible, it is clear that not even a
political dreamer could seriously consider the feasi-
bility of a genuine popular election. From what I
know of many of the inhabitants, from what I have
seen of their complete indifference to anything out-

side of their villages and cornfields, I think it highly probable that many thousands of them tilled their land throughout the entire, futile "reign" altogether unaware of Maximilian's existence. Maximilian was not elected Emperor of Mexico by popular vote, although before he learned something about his empire, he no doubt thought he had been.

As to the second condition—when Maximilian staked his entire hope of success upon a promise of Napoleon III, who had on various occasions somewhat conspicuously shown himself to be as dangerous an adventurer and as unscrupulous a liar as most of the other members of his offensive family, Maximilian did something that may be recorded as trusting and unfortunate, but that is only adequately described as dull. Fatuous, ignorant, and dull, he not only failed to pull out Napoleon's chestnuts, he proceeded to fall into the fire. Except just at first, he was not wanted in Mexico even by the clerical party responsible for his being there; for his refusal to abolish the Reform Laws and restore the power of the Church bitterly disappointed the Church without, however, gaining for him adherents among those who had fought so long to establish a republic. Everything he did was preordained to be wrong. He went without a definite policy and was incapable of evolving one after he arrived. His three years in Mexico were unproductive of anything except an enormous debt incurred largely by the silly magnificence of his court, a great deal of bloodshed and his own execution. He died bravely, one always reads, but so do hundreds of other persons every day. Before an audience composed of the entire civilized world, to die bravely ought not to be a particularly difficult feat. As Alphonse Daudet somewhere says of Frenchmen, " They can always be brave if there are enough people looking." Life was not kind to the young Austrian, but history has been.

And yet, on the sad, silent terraces of the Jardin Borda one always thinks of Maximilian and Carlotta, and pays them the tribute of a sentimental pang.

XV

TRAVELERS sometimes complain that "Mexican towns are exactly alike; if you see one you've seen them all," and while I cannot agree with the bromidically couched observation I can understand why it is made. They are not alike, but they are so startlingly different from Northern towns that one is at first more impressed by this fundamental difference, in which they all naturally have a family resemblance, than by the less striking but delightful ways in which they often differ from one another. Without exception, they are, as art critics used to say of certain pictures, "painted in a high key," and where the nature of the site permits, their rectangularity is positively Philadelphian. In their center is a public square with a garden, rather formal in intention but as a rule old enough and luxuriant enough to have lost its original stiffness. Here there are paths and benches, trees, fountains, flowers, and a flimsy looking iron and tin band stand one learns at last to like. At one side is the most important church; the other

three are bounded by shops and arcades. This is
the plaza. Every town has one, many of them have
several. But there is always one that more than the
others is a kind of pulsating, civic heart, and it is interesting to note how in their dimensions they observe the scale of their environment. Big towns have
big plazas, small towns have small plazas, villages
have tiny plazas. In addition to the plaza there is
often, in a quieter, more distant quarter of the community, a park—a tangled, shady, bird-inhabited
spot, with high and aged trees, massive seats of stone
or cement, and a tranquillity that exerts a noticeably
benign influence on all who go to walk or sit there.
Whether the houses and buildings are built of stone
or mortar or, as is customary in the smaller places
of the plateau, of sun-dried mud bricks, their effect
is the same, for they are all given a coat of smooth
stucco and then calcimined white, or a pale shade of
pink, blue, yellow, buff, or green. Rarely are they
of more than two stories; most of them have balconies on the upper floor, all have long, heavily
barred windows on the lower, and if it were not for
their gayety of color, the perpetual fascination of
their flower-filled patios of which the passer-by gets
tantalizing glimpses through open doorways, and the
intellectual interest of the signs on the shops—their

uniform height and the square simplicity of their design might be monotonous. As it is, a Mexican street, even when empty, is never monotonous.

Besides the plaza and the park, there is the market place—sometimes merely an open square in which the venders, under rectangular homemade parasols, spread their wares upon the ground, but more often an inclosure equipped with long counters and protected from sun and rain by a roof. Except in the City of Mexico, Guadalajara, and Merida, one is not conscious of " residence quarters." The " best families " (a term almost as meaningless and as frequently employed in Mexico as in the United States) live where they please, and they please to live as deeply as possible in the thick of things. The largest and most elaborate houses are often scattered between shops and saloons along the busiest streets, and when one becomes intimate with the country and its inhabitants it seems natural and agreeable that they should be. For one cannot live in Mexico without consciously or unconsciously regarding the superficialities of life from something very like the local point of view. There is about it an infectious and inevitable quality, and I have often been both amused and depressed by the manner in which foreigners who accept the best of everything in Mexico—who grow strong, and revel in one of its several climates, who make a good living there, who enjoy its beauty and adopt many of its customs—stupidly deny its attraction for them, repudiate their sympathy with it. It is customary, almost a convention, to do so, and one is appalled by the tenacity of convention's grasp upon the ordinary mind—by the impregnable dullness of the normal intellect. I know, for example, Americans who have lived happily in Mexico for many years. They have, among Mexicans, friends whom they both respect and admire. Almost all their interests in life are focused somewhere in the country, and when they are away from it they look forward with gladness to the time of their return. Yet, apparent as all this is to one who associates with them, they seem incapable of translating experience into consciousness and conversation. You see them leading contented and successful lives, at peace with their adopted land and almost everything in it; but when they undertake to discuss their environment, to formulate their opinions, their remarks are rarely valuable and never appreciative. Instead of simply trying to give one something of the Mexico they have day by day, month by month, and year by year met and succumbed to, they appear to take a pride in parading the old geography, guidebook and tourist dicta that in their cases, one sees at a glance, are not justified by facts.

"All Mexican servants are thieves and liars," is the characteristic pronouncement of an American woman whose household for sixteen years has been admirably and economically run by the same devoted and honest cook.

"What a filthy lot they are!" exclaims her husband (who observes the good old custom of taking a bath every Saturday night whether he needs it or not), as we ride through a Yucatecan village in which most of the Indian inhabitants scrub from head to foot and put on clean clothes every day.

"I wouldn't trust one of them with a cent," declares some one else, who has in his office three Mexican clerks to whom he implicitly intrusts the handling of thousands of dollars.

"I look upon them just as I look upon niggers," says a Southerner—who not only doesn't, but who is gratified by the pleasant position he has achieved for himself in local, native society. And as such comments are made with neither malicious intent nor with the "feeling" that would accompany them were they final deductions from a long series of painful experiences, one marvels at the phonographic monotony with which they are endlessly reproduced.

Almost always purely verbal, there is behind them neither thought nor emotion, and they are irritating in much the same way that checks are irritating when carelessly made out and signed by persons who have nothing in the bank. They are, I fancy, connected with a sense of patriotism that has grown habitual and perfunctory, and I mention them merely by way of illustrating half of my assertion to the effect that one absorbs something of Mexico both unconsciously and with deliberateness. A young Englishman of my acquaintance may well supply the other half.

It is not generally realized that the male inhabitants of Great Britain do not make a practice of wearing drawers, although such is the strange, dissembled fact. Now, while the possession of underclothes is not necessarily indicative of birth and wealth, I have always assumed, although perhaps with a certain apathy, that the possession of wealth and birth presupposed underclothes. This, in England at least, does not seem to be the case, for my young friend, whose name is ancient and whose purse is well filled, announced to me in Mexico not long ago, with the naïveté that so often asto..'shes one in thoroughly sophisticated persons of his race: " I've knocked about a good bit and I've come to the conclusion that there's usually something to be said for the peculiar habits of different peoples even if you don't know exactly what it is. Since I've been in this country I've noticed that everybody seems to wear drawers—even the peons. There must be some reason for it—connected with the climate very likely —and I've taken to wearing them myself. I don't particularly care for the things," he hastened apolo⁓ getically to add, " and I dare say they're all rot, but I'm going to give them a try. Why don't you!"

It is natural and agreeable in Mexico to have one's house in what we call " the retail district," for one soon learns to appreciate the Mexican's combined love of seclusion and publicity. A dwelling sand- wiched in between the town's most popular drug and grocery shops is ideally situated. The nature of its construction—the Moors imposed it upon Spain and Spain passed it on—insures a fortresslike priv- acy, while the site insures the constant movement and color, the manifold, trivial, human and animal in- terests without which the life of a Mexican house- hold would be somewhat empty. Those odd mo- ments consumed by us with magazines and the book of the week, Mexicans devote to looking out of their sala windows, with a rarely misplaced confidence in their street's potentialities. It never strikes me as strange that *I* can pass so many hours in peering at sights so foreign to my race, if not any longer to my experience, but it is one of the pleasantly surprising traits of the inhabitants that *their* interest is just as fresh and perhaps more insatiable. To me the love affair across the way—carried on as it is with much holding of hands in the excessive broadness of Mexican daylight, by a young woman of thirty-eight behind a barred window, and a young man of forty-two on the narrow sidewalk outside—to me, this public display of an emotion, ordinarily regarded as rather private, is most exciting; but even so, I am inclined to believe that after commenting on such a courtship every afternoon and evening for three and a half years it would begin to pall. On Mexicans it never seems to. They do not precisely stare at the spectacle, as a careful unawareness under the circumstances is considered the proper line to take. But their blind spots are not situated in the tails of their eyes. However, it does not necessitate such absorbing matters as affairs of the heart to retain their attention. They never weary at certain hours of the day of peering through the bars or leaning over the balconies in contemplation of just the street's multifarious but always leisurely movement. It is not often a noisy movement. The collective

Mexican voice—the voice of a group or even a crowd is musical, and the click of donkey's hoofs on cobblestones is a dainty, a positively prim form of commotion.

But should they wish to escape from even these sometimes distinctly soothing sounds, there is always the patio and the tranquil rooms around it. They are of all sizes, of all degrees of misery and splendor and of most shapes, these universal patios, but in the meanest of them there is an expressed yearning for color and adornment that, even when ill cared for and squalid, has been at least expressed. It takes the form, most fortunately, of flowers, with often a fountain in a circular basin of blue and white tiles. A Mexican patio, in fact, is considerably more than a courtyard. It is a flower garden surrounded by a house.

In Northern climates the most delightful hour of the day has always been that in which one comes in from the frosty dusk, lights the lamps, smashes a smoldering lump of coal into a bright, sudden blaze, draws the curtain and, in an atmosphere thick with warmth and quiet, sits down to read or write or rest. In tropical countries one often longs in vain for this hour. Its impossibility is, I think, a chief cause of homesickness, and it is long before one ac-

cepts with anything like the same sense—a sense
of physical and mental well-being immune from
gazes and intrusions—the Southern equivalent. The
Southern equivalent is the hour in which the sun
shines brightest and fiercest, when instead of seeking warmth one eludes it, half undressed, in dim,
bare rooms, under awnings and behind light, thin
screens.

Even when a street for the time being comparatively lacks moving figures there is for the foreigner
a constant amusement in reading the signs over the
doors of shops and more especially those that decorate
the outer walls of pulque joints and cantinas. Their
mere perusal, indeed, may throw a truer, more valuable light upon certain phases of the native humors
and habits of thought than do many works less spon-
taneous and more profound. "Jack O'Grady,
Sample Room," or, "Otto Baumholzer, Saloon,"
may or may not make an appeal. But even when it
does it is not an appeal to the intellect and the imagination. In Mexico the proprietor of a saloon likes
to advertise his wares, not so much with his name
as with a sentiment, an allusion—a word or a phrase
that poetically connotes. There are of course a
great many serviceable designations of no particular
relevance like the patriotic "Cinco de Mayo," the

inevitable "Estrella de Oro," and the frequently
met with and rather meaningless "Cometa de 1843."
They show respectively only a taste for the national,
the brilliant, the surprising. The gift of fancy is
not, after all, to everyone. Even when a foul little
corner drunkery, calcimined sky-blue—with a life-
sized lady reposing in a green bower, painted on
its finger-marked exterior—is entitled " El Nido de
Amor," or when a pink hole in the wall that can
be seen for a block and smelled for two, is named
" Las Flores de Abril "—even then one does not appreciate quite to the full some of the quaint possibilities of just the ordinary Mexican mind. But a
saloon called " El Destino," another frankly advertising itself as " La Isla de Sacrificios," still another
with painted above its door " El Infiernito " (the
little hell), a fourth that calls itself " Al Delirio "—
there is in such names food, as one strolls about any
Mexican community, for meditation. Less grim,
but as suggestive and as apt, is " La Seductora."
" La Media Noche " and " Las Aves de la Noche "
(the night birds) always strike a sympathetic chord,
while " El Renacimiento," " El Valor," and " El
Mensajero de los Dioses " (the messenger of the
gods) gracefully hoist the whole matter into the
realm of the ideal. The subtlest of them, and the

one that never fails to make me laugh as I pass it, is " La Idea! " I regret now that the opportunity of entering and making the proprietor's acquaintance has gone. A man who would name his saloon " La Idea! " ought to be worth knowing. The thing can be apperceived in so many ways and spoken in so many different tones of voice, starting, as at once suggests itself, with the intonation generally imparted to, " Why, the idea! "

One source of dissatisfaction to travelers for whom foreign travel has always meant Europe, is that there are so few " sights " in Mexican towns. By " sights " I mean the galleries of sculpture and painting, the palaces and the castles, the frescoes, the architectural fragments, the tombs, the relics, and the interminable museums crammed with a dead world's junk, over which the conscientious may exhaust their necks and backs. European cities even as comparatively small as Stockholm and Copenhagen possess museums where, guidebook in hand, people remain for whole days examining ugly, labeled little implements fashioned in the stone age, the bronze age, the iron age, and every city has among other treasures a few miles of minute, Dutch masters before which to trudge, too weary to appreciate their marvelous skill or to realize their

beauty. But in Mexican towns there are none of
these things, and the traveler whose days have not
been mapped out for him and who is not in the habit
of strolling, of sitting in churches, of shamelessly
idling in parks and plazas, is likely to complain of
a lack of occupation. It is difficult for him to accept the fact that the most notable sight in Mexico
is simply Mexico.

It is difficult, too, for him to reconcile the general
outward conditions of the towns and cities with his
preconceived ideas of them, which is always annoying. Instead of giving an impression of dirt and
neglect, of the repulsive indifference to appearances,
and general "shiftlessness" we are so accustomed
to in the small communities of States like, for instance, Arkansas and Indiana, their best quarters always, and their more modest districts very often, are
perpetually swept and sprinkled, dazzling with new
calcimine and, for thoroughfares so aged, incredibly
neat and gay. About drainage and water works—
the invisible and important—there is still much to
deplore, much to hope for, although improvement is
everywhere on the way. But municipal "appearances" are rigidly maintained; maintained in some
instances at the cost, unfortunately, of qualities that
share the secret of the country's charm. There is

at the present time, for example, a rage—a madness rather—for renovating, for " doing over " the exteriors of churches, and in the last four years some of the most impressive examples of Spanish colonial church architecture have been scraped, punctured with pointed windows, supplied with gargoyles and porticoes and then whitewashed. To remember the cathedral at Jalapa as it was, and to see it now, a jaunty horror half clad in cheap, Gothic clothes that don't fit, brings a lump to one's throat.

The order and security that everywhere appear to reign both by day and by night are also bewildering in a country popularly supposed to be the modern fountain-head of lawlessness and melodrama. Besides the small but businesslike policemen with large, visible revolvers who seem to be on every corner and who materialize in swarms at the slightest infringement of the code, the highways are patrolled by that picturesque body of men known as rurales, of whom there are between four and five thousand. After the fall of Santa Anna, the organized troop of ranchmen (known as " cuerados " from the leather clothes they wore) became bandits and gained for themselves the name of " plateados," it being their dashing custom heavily to ornament their garments with silver. In the time of Comonfort they were turned from their evil ways (no doubt on the theory of its taking a thief to catch a thief) and transformed into rurales. Under President Diaz they have attained a high degree of efficiency, and while their practically limitless powers in isolated and inaccessible parts of the country are no doubt sometimes abused, their reputation for fearlessness, supplemented by a revolver, a carbine, and a saber, has a most chastening influence. One realizes something of the number of policemen at night, when they deposit their lighted lanterns in the middle of the streets and there is until dawn a ceaseless concert of their wailing whistles. You may become as drunk as you wish to in a cantina and, even with the doors open, talk as loud and as long as you are able, for cantinas were made to get drunk and talk loud in. But you must walk quite steadily when you come out—unless your wife or daughter is laughingly leading you home—or you will be arrested before you reel ten yards. Even chaperoned by your wife and unmistakably homeward bound, you will be escorted kindly, almost gently (when you show no resistance), to the police station if the city happens to need your services. The combination of quick temper and quicker drink is responsible for much violence in Mexico, but one rarely sees it. One rarely sees any form of disorder, and over vice is draped a cloak of complete invisibility. In most places women of the town are not even permitted to appear on the streets except at certain hours and in a capacity sincerely unprofessional. The facility and dispatch with which one is arrested is conducive to a constant appearance of decorum. Only in a paternal despotism is such law and order possible. One evening I myself was arrested for an exceedingly slight and innocent midemeanor.

" But why do you arrest me? Why don't you arrest everybody else? I'm not the only one," I protested to the policeman with a lightness I was beginning not to feel.

" You are a foreigner and a gentleman and you ought to set an example to the ignorant lower classes," he replied without a smile. It was some time before I could induce him to let me go.

The frequency of the policemen is equaled (or exceeded, one sometimes feels) only by the frequency of the churches. And, as if there were not already thousands more than the souls of any people could possibly need, new ones are always being built. I was told not long ago of a wealthy man who, on recently acquiring a vast area of land which he contemplated turning into a sugar hacienda, began the construction of his "plant" with a thirty-thousand-dollar church. Their number and the manner in which they monopolize all the most conspicuous sites, as well as render conspicuous most of the others, now and then enables even a Roman Catholic to regard the Laws of Reform with a slightly less bilious eye. The countryside is dotted with them—the towns and cities crowded by them. It seems at times as if the streets were but so many convenient lanes through which to approach them— the shops and houses merely so many modest dependencies. Pictorially considered, they imbue the dreariest most impersonal of landscapes, especially just after sunset, with a mild and lovely atmosphere of human pathos that one might journey far without seeing again. But even in Mexico the pictorial sense is subject to periods of suspended animation during which one's attitude toward the churches, or perhaps I should say the Church, is curiously ill-defined. It is discomposing, on the one hand, to learn of a powerful bishop whose "wife" and large family of sons and daughters are complacently taken for granted by his entire diocese—to be warned by a devout Catholic never under any circumstances to allow one's American maid servants to converse with a priest or to enter his house on any pretext whatever

—to appreciate the extreme poverty of the people and to realize that the entire gigantic corporation is kept running chiefly by the hard-earned mites with which they hope to save their souls. In the church of San Miguel (not a particularly large church) at Orizaba, I once had the curiosity to count the various devices by which the faithful are hypnotized into leaving their money behind them, and as I made notes of the little alms boxes in front of all the chapels, at the doors, and scattered along the nave, many of them with a placard explaining the use to which the funds were supposed to be put, I could not but admire the unerring instinct with which the emotions of the race had been gauged. The system, assisted as it is by a fantastically dressed lay figure at every placarded box, has for the population of Orizaba (an excessively religious town) much the same fascination that is exercised upon me by a penny arcade. There were boxes for " The Monthly Mass of Jesus," " For the Marble Cross," " For the Sick," " For the Sick of S. Vincent and S. Paul," " For Mary Conceived without Sin," " For Our Father Jesus Carrying the Cross," " For Saint Michael," " For the Blessed Souls," " For the Blessed Virgin," " For Our Lady of Carmen," and then, as if the ground had not been tolerably well covered, there were two boxes, " For the Work of this Parish." But these were literally less than half the total number. In addition to the twelve whose uses were revealed, there were *eighteen others* whose uses were not, or thirty in all.

On the other hand, I cannot linger in Mexican churches day after day, as I have done, watching the Indians glide in, remove the leather bands from their foreheads, let their chitas slip gently to the pavement, and then, with straight backs and crossed hands, kneel in reverent ecstasy before their favorite images, without rejoicing that a profound human want can be so filled to overflowing. And I cannot but doubt that it could by any other way we know be filled at all. Three men in Indian white, who are returning from market to their homes in some distant village, stop to kneel for fully half an hour without moving before the chapel of St. Michael. St. Michael happens to be an almost life-sized female doll with pink silk socks, the stiff skirts of a ballet-dancer (actually), a pink satin bolero jacket, an imitation diamond necklace, a blond wig with long curls, and a tin helmet. The two women who accompany them pray before the figure of Mary Conceived without Sin—whose costume I prefer not to invite the accusation of sacrilege by recording. The men are straight-backed, motionless, enthralled. One of the women suddenly extends her arms with an all-embracing gesture, and rigidly holds them there—her hands palm upward, as if she expected to receive the stigmata. What are they all thinking about? But what earthly difference does it make—if there be a difference so heavenly? No doubt they are thinking of nothing; thought is not essential to bliss. Then they get up, and after dropping money in the little slot machines of Michael, and Mary Conceived without Sin, they proceed on their way, leaving me glad that for fully half an hour some one in the world has been happy. For beyond the possibility of a doubt they have been happy, and have deepened my conviction that the desire to undermine their faith in Michael and in Mary Conceived without Sin is at best misguided, and at worst, wicked. "Idolatry and superstition!" one hears groaned from end to end of Mexico. But why not? They appear to be very comforting, exalting things. It happens that personally I could derive no spiritual refreshment from remaining on my knees for half an hour in front of these dreadful dolls. But there is a statue or two in the Louvre, and several pictures in Florence, to whom—had I been brought up to believe them capable of performing miracles—I should find it most agreeable and beneficial to say my prayers.

So one's attitude toward the Church in Mexico becomes at the last curiously ill-defined. The Church is corrupt, grasping, resentful; but it unquestionably gives millions of people something without which they would be far more unhappy than they are—something that no other church could give them.

There are city parks and squares in other countries, but in none do they play the same intimate and important part in the national domestic life that they do in Mexico. To one accustomed to associate the " breathing spaces " with red-nosed tramps and collarless, unemployed men dejectedly reading wilted newspapers on shabby benches, it would be impossible to give an idea of what the plaza means to the people of Mexico—of how it is used by them. It strikes me always as a kind of open-air drawing-room, not only, as are our own public squares, free to all, but, unlike them, frequented by all. It is not easy to imagine one's acquaintances in the United States putting on their best clothes for the purpose of strolling around and around the public square of even one of the smaller cities, to the efforts of a brass band, however good; but in Mexico one's acquaintances take an indescribable amount of innocent pleasure in doing just this on three evenings a week and on Sunday afternoons as well. And with a simplicity—a democracy—that is a strange contradiction in a people who have inherited so much punctilio—such pride of position, they do it together with all the servants and laborers in town. In the smaller places the men at these concerts promenade in one direction, while the women, and the women accompanied by men, revolve in the other; a convenient arrangement that permits the men to apperceive the charms of the women, and the women to apperceive the charms of the men without effort or boldness on the part of either. And everyone is socially so at ease! There is among the rich and well dressed not the slightest trace of that " certain condescension " observable, I feel sure, when the duke and the duchess graciously pair off with the housekeeper and the butler, and among the lower classes—the maid and men servants, the stone-masons and carpenters, the cargadores, the clerks, the small shopkeepers—there is neither the aggressive sense of an equality that does not exist nor a suggestion of servility. The sons of, say, the governor of the state, and their com-

panions, will stroll away the evening between two
groups of sandaled Indians with blankets on their
shoulders—his daughters in the midst of a phalanx
of laundresses and cooks; the proximity being carried off with an engaging naturalness, an apparent
unawareness of difference on the part of everyone
that is the perfection of good manners. When such
contacts happen with us it is invariably an experiment, never a matter of course. Our upper classes
self-consciously regard themselves as doing something rather quaint—experiencing a new sensation,
while the lower classes eye them with mixed emotions I have never been able satisfactorily to analyze.

But the serenatas are the least of it. The
plaza is in constant use from morning until late at
night. Ladies stop there on their way home from
church, " dar una vuelta " (to take a turn), as they
call it, and to see and be seen; gentlemen frequently
interrupt the labors of the day by going there to
meditate over a cigar; schoolboys find in it a shady,
secluded bench and use it as a study; nurse maids
use it as a nursery; children use its broad, outside
walks as a playground; tired workmen use it as a
place of rest. By eleven o'clock at night the whole
town will, at various hours, have passed through it,
strolled in it, played, sat, rested, talked, or thought

in it. It is the place to go when in doubt as to what to do with oneself—the place to investigate, when in doubt as to where to find some one. The plaza is a kind of social clearing house—a resource—a solution. I know of nothing quite like it, and nothing as fertile in the possibilities of innocent diversion. Except during a downpour of rain, the plaza never disappoints.

I have grown rather tired of reading in magazines that " the City of Mexico resembles a bit of Paris "; but I have grown much more tired of the people who have also read it and repeat it as if they had evolved the comparison unaided—particularly as the City of Mexico doesn't in the least resemble a bit of Paris. It resembles absolutely nothing in the world except itself. To criticise it as having most of the objectionable features and few of the attractions of a great city would be unfair; but first telling myself that I *am* unfair, I always think of it in those terms. In truth it is a great and wonderful city, and it grows more wonderful every day; also, I am inclined to believe, more disagreeable. Unfortunately I did not see it until after I had spent six months in Mexico—in Vera Cruz, in Jalapa, in Orizaba, in Puebla, in the depths of the country—and when it finally burst upon me in all its shallow brilliancy, I felt that I was no longer in Mexico, but without the compensation of seeming to be somewhere else. I certainly did not seem to be in Paris. The fact of going to a place for no reason other than to see what it is like, always stands between me and a proper appreciation of it. It does, I think, with everyone, although it is not generally realized and admitted. A certain amount of preoccuption while visiting a city is essential to receiving just impressions of it. The formation of judgments should be gradual and unconscious—should resemble the processes of digestion. I have been in the capital of the republic half a dozen times, but I have never, so to speak, digested it; I have merely looked without losing consciousness of the fact that I was looking, which is conducive to seeing too much on the one hand, and on the other, too little.

After the jungle and the smaller places, the city impressed me, on arriving at night, as wonderfully brilliant. There were asphalted streets, vistas of illuminated shop windows, enormous electric cars, the inviting glow of theater entrances, a frantic darting of cabs and automobiles, and swarms of people in a strangely un-Mexican hurry. The noises and the lights were the noises and the lights

of a metropolis. Even daylight did not, for the
first morning and afternoon, have any appreciable
effect upon the general sense of size and effulgence.
But somewhere within forty-eight hours the place,
to a mere observer, began to contract—its glitter
became increasingly difficult to discern. It was not
a disappointment exactly, but neither was it " just
like a bit of Paris." It remained extremely interesting—geographically, historically, architecturally
—but it was oddly lacking in the one quality everybody is led to believe it has in a superlative degree.
Without doubt I shall be thought trifling to mention it at all. In fact I don't believe I *can* mention it, as I don't precisely know what it is, and the
only way in which I can hope to make myself even
partly clear will sound not only trifling but foolish.
I mean—the City of Mexico lacks the indefinable
quality that makes one either desirous of putting
on one's best clothes, or regretful that one has not
better clothes to put on. To dear reader this
may mean something or it may not. For me it instantly recreates an atmosphere, recalls certain
streets at certain hours in New York, in Paris, in
London—in a few of the less down-at-the-heel,
Congoesque localities of Washington. One may or
may not possess the garments in question. One

might not take the trouble to put them on if one
did. But the feeling, I am sure, is known to everyone; the feeling that in some places there is a
pleasantly exacting standard in the amenities of appearance which one must either approximate, or remain an outsider. In the City of Mexico one is
nowhere subject to such aspirations or misgivings,
in spite of the "palatial residences," the superb
horses, the weekly display of beauty and fashion.
For the place has upon one—it has at least upon me
—the effect of something new and indeterminate
and mongrel, which for a city founded in 1522 is
a decidedly curious effect to exert.

It arises without doubt from the prosperity and
growth of the place—the manner in which it is
tearing down and building up and reaching out—
gradually transforming whole streets of old Spanish and Mexican houses into buildings that are
modern and heterogeneous. In its center, some five
or six adjacent streets appear to have been almost
wholly so converted, the final proof of it being that
in front of the occasional elaborately carved old
doorway or armorial-bearing façade and castellated
top, one instinctively pauses as in the presence of
a curiosity. Imbedded as they are in unusually un-
attractive quarters of purely native origin, these half

a dozen business streets suggest a small city in the heart of a large town. They might, one feels, be somewhere in Europe, although the multitude of American signs, of American products, and American residents, by which one is on all sides confronted, makes it impossible to decide where. There is a surprising transformation, too, on the left of the Paseo, along the line of the electric cars on the way to the castle of Chapultepec. (A lady in the throes of displaying an interest in Mexico exclaimed to me the other day: " There have been so many earthquakes in Mexico of late that I suppose Chapultepec is *very* active! ") The bare, flat territory is growing an enormous crop of detached dwellings that seek to superimpose Mexican characteristics upon an American suburban-villa foundation, with results not always felicitous. Outwardly, at least, much of the city is being de-Mexicanized, and whereas the traveler, to whom it has been a gate of entrance, has eyes and adjectives only for its age, its singularity, its picturesqueness (all of which are indisputably there), the traveler who sees it last—for whom it is an exit—is more inclined merely to be discomposed by its uncompleted modernity.

For, not unreasonably, he expects to find there

some of the frills of civilization; luxurious hotels, "smart" restaurants, an embarrassing choice of cafés and theaters. Such frills as there are, however, succeed for the most part in being only pretentious and ineffective, like those a woman tries to make at home after taking notes in front of a milliner's window. The leading hotels are all bad—not in the sense of being uncomfortable, for they are comfortable enough, but in the sense of purporting to be something they are not. The four I have stayed in reminded me of a placard I once saw while endeavoring to find something edible at a railway "eating house" in one of our Western States. "Low Aim, not Failure is a Crime," the thing declared with an almost audible snigger. Surrounded by the second- and third-rate magnificence of the capital's best hotels, one longs for the clean, native simplicity of the provinces. The theaters—that is to say, what one hears and sees in them—are quite as primitive and tedious as they are elsewhere. A translated French play now and then proves a temptation, but as it is customary in Mexican theaters for the prompter to read everybody's part, whether he needs assistance or not, in a voice as loud and often louder than those of the actors, the pleasure of illusion is out of the question. In fact, it is such a matter of course for the prompter to yell through a whole play at the top of his lungs (often reading the lines *after* the actors instead of ahead of them), that when, as happens once in a long while, his services are dispensed with, the fact is proudly advertised! I have several times gleaned from the advance notices of traveling companies that on such and such a night Señorita So-and-So would take the leading part in the laughable comedy entitled "'Thingumbob,' sin auxilio de apuntador!" (without the aid of the prompter.) Nothing in connection with the theater in Mexico has seemed to me more entertaining than this, unless, perhaps, it is that at the Teatro Limón in Jalapa, "The management respectfully requests gentlemen not to bring their firearms to the performances." Whether or not this plaintive plea is on the principle of the old "Don't shoot the organist; he is doing his best," I have never been able to learn.

There are saloons in the City of Mexico, hundreds of them, but cafés of the kind that are such oases in the evenings of France, of Germany, of Italy, have not (with the exception of the delightful one at the base of Chapultepec, which, however, is several miles out of town) yet been invented. In the matter of restaurants (again excepting the distant Chapultepec) there is no choice whatever, if one happens to be in the mood to draw a distinction between eating and dining. People talk of the food at the various hotels, but when speaking of Sylvain's restaurant they elegantly refer to the *cuisine*. Sylvain's is a small, quiet, dignified, almost somber place where everything, except occasionally the service, is as wickedly good as it is anywhere in the world, and where the cost of painting the culinary lily is somewhat less than it is in establishments of similar excellence in New York (I know of none in the United States outside of New York) and Europe.

But taking the city as it is (always a sane and sensible line of action) rather than finding fault with it for not being what one assumed it was going to be, it has its moments—moments that, as far as my experience permits me to speak with a semblance of authority, are peculiar to itself. On Sunday mornings three beautiful allées of the Alameda are lined with little chairs and roofed with gayly decorated canvas, under which the world and his wife sit, or very slowly promenade down one side and up the other in two densely crowded, music-loving streams. It is a variation of the plaza idea of the smaller places, the variation consisting in the aloofness of the classes from the masses. And by the masses in the capital is usually meant, although the distinction is a loose one, persons who still wear native costume. A cheap, ill-fitting suit of American cut is a passport to a slightly higher position in the social scale—which somewhat shoddy conception was responsible a year ago for the abolishment of the sombreros worn by cabmen. Until then, these towers of protection had imparted to cabstands the character and distinction possessed by no other form of head covering. But now, no livery having been substituted, the drivers wear dingy felt hats, and carry battered umbrellas when obliged to sit in the sun.

The band is very large and very good—so large and good, indeed, that later in the day, at four or five o'clock, as one joins the ever-increasing throng of carriages, cabs, and automobiles on the Paseo, one is amazed to discover several others even larger and better, playing in the magnificent circular glorietas along the drive to Chapultepec. In the park at the Paseo's farther end is still another, and whether it actually does play with more flexibility, feeling, and taste than the bands I have heard in other countries, or whether the romantic beauty of the situation —the dusky cypress grove, the steep, craggy rock,

288

literally dripping with flowers, from which the castle
smiles down at the crowd (it belongs to the smiling,
not the frowning family of castles) the gleam of the
lake through aged trees, the happy compromise between wildness and cultivation—weaves the spell,
transmutes brass into gold, I do not know. The
Paseo was begun during the French intervention,
and although its trees and its statues of national
celebrities are alike small for its splendid breadth
(the trees, however, will grow), too much could not
be said in praise of the conception itself, and the
manner in which it has been carried out. It is one
of the noblest of avenues and, with the Alameda
at one end and the gardens of Chapultepec at the
other, does much in the City of Mexico to make
life worth living there.

The crowd of vehicles increases until there is a
compact slow-moving mass of them creeping past
the band stand, into the cypress grove, around the
other side of the park and back again. Many of
the carriages are victorias and landaus of the latest
design, the horses drawing them are superb, the lady
occupants are always elaborately dressed and sometimes notably handsome. So it is odd that most
of this wealth and fashion and beauty seems to shy
at servants in livery. There are equipages with

" two men on the box," complete in every detail, but in the endless jam of vehicles their number is small. That there are not more of them seems especially remiss after one has seen the few. For in English livery a young and good-looking Mexican servant exemplifies more than any other human being the thing called " style." As darkness comes on everyone returns to town to drive in San Francisco Street until half past eight or nine. This is a most extraordinary sight—the narrow thoroughfare in the heart of the city so congested with carriages as to be more or less impassable for two hours —the occupants under the electric lights more pallid than their powder—the sidewalks packed with spectators constantly urged by the police to " move on." It all happens at the same hour every Sunday, and no one seems to tire.

When I said there were but few " sights " in Mexican cities I made, in the case of the capital, a mental reservation. Here there are formal, official, objective points sufficient to keep the intelligent tourist busy for a week; the cathedral, the Viga canal, the shrine of Guadalupe, the Monte de Piedad—the National Palace, and the Castle of Chapultepec, if one cares to measure the red tape necessary to passing within their historic and deeply interesting portals. Even if one doesn't, it would, in my opinion, be a tragedy to leave without seeing, at sunset, the view of the volcanoes from the top of the rock on which the castle is built; especially as this can be done by following, without a card of admission, the steep, winding road past the pretty grottolike entrance to the President's elevator, until it ends at the gateway of the famous military school on the summit. One also goes, of course, to the National Museum to inspect the small but immensely valuable collection of Aztec remains (large compared to any other Aztec remains, but small, if one pauses to recall the remains in general that have remained elsewhere) and to receive the impression that the pre-Spanish inhabitants of the country, interesting as they undoubtedly were, had by no means attained that facility in the various arts which Prescott and other historians claim for them. After examining their grotesque and terrifying gods, the incoherent calendar and sacrificial stones, the pottery, the implements, and the few bits of crude, gold jewelry, one strolls into the small room in which are left, perhaps, the most tangible evidences of Maximilian's " empire," reflecting that Prescott's monumental effort is one of the most entrancing works of fiction one knows. To the unarcheological, Maximilian's state coach, almost as overwhelmingly magnificent as the gilded sledge in which Lillian Russell used to make her entrance in " The Grand Duchess," his carriage for ordinary occasions, the saddle he was in when captured, and the colored fashion plates of his servants' liveries, are sure to be the museum's most interesting possessions. Not without a pardonable touch of malice, in the guise of a grave political lesson, is the fact that the severely simple, well-worn, eminently republican vehicle of Benito Juarez is displayed in the same room.

The four or five vast apartments of the Academy of San Carlos (the national picture gallery) suggests certain aspects of the Louvre, but their variously sized canvases suggest only the melancholy reflection that all over the world so many perfectly well-painted pictures are so perfectly uninteresting. One cannot but except, however, a dozen or more scattered little landscapes—absolutely faultless examples of the kind of picture (a very beautiful kind I have grown to think) that the grandparents of all good Bostonians felt it becoming their means and station to acquire fifty or sixty years ago in Rome. The Mexican Government, it no doubt will be surprising to hear, encourages painting and music by substantial scholarships. Talented students are sent abroad to study at government expense. One young man I happened to know was given his opportunity on the strength of an exquisite oil sketch of the patio of his parents' house in the white glare of noon. He is in Paris now, painting pictures of naked women lying on their backs in vacant lots. Several of them, naturally, have been hung in the Salon.

But the guidebook will enumerate the sights, and the " Seeing Mexico " electric car will take one to them. Still there is one I do not believe the book mentions, and I am sure the car does not include. That is the city itself between five and six o'clock on a fair morning. It several times has been my good fortune (in disguise) to be obliged to get up at this hour for the purpose of saying good-by to people who were leaving on an early train, and in returning all the way on foot from the station to the Zócalo (as the stupendous square in front of the cathedral is called) I saw the place, I am happy to remember, in what was literally as well as figuratively a new light. Beyond a few laborers straggling to their work, and the men who were making the toilet of the Alameda with large, green bushes attached to the end of sticks, the city appeared to be

293

blandly slumbering, and just as the face of some one we know will, while asleep, surprise us by a rare and unsuspected expression, the great, unfinished, unsympathetic capital smiled, wisely and a trifle wearily, in its dreams. It is at this hour, before the mongrel population has begun to swarm, that one should walk through the Alameda, inhale the first freshness of the wet roses and lilies, the gardenias and pansies and heliotrope in the flower market, and, undisturbed among the trees in front of the majestic cathedral, listen to " the echoed sob of history."

(5)

THE END

Previously published by
ELAND BOOKS

A DRAGON APPARENT

One of the most absorbing travel books I have read for a very
long time... the great charm of the work is its literary vividness.
Nothing he describes is dull, and he writes as entertainingly of a
Saigon nightclub as of the stupendous ruins of Angkor, and the
flowers and birds in a forest clearing.
Peter Quennell, Daily Mail

To Indo-China Mr Norman Lewis took the equipment of a
sensitive Englishman with a coolly yet sympathetically critical
eye and a catholic taste. With that he joined the ability, manifest
on every page of *A Dragon Apparent*, to write a sustainedly
evocative prose.
Daily Telegraph

A book which should take its place in the permanent literature of
the Far East.
Economist

A brilliant report on a period of violent transition in a strange
land... *A Dragon Apparent* is a very good book indeed.
Peter Fleming, Spectator

REVIEWS OF OTHER TRAVEL BOOKS
BY NORMAN LEWIS

Mr Lewis can make even a lorry interesting.
Cyril Connolly, Sunday Times

He really goes in deep like a polished knife. I have never travelled
in my life so fast, variously and well.
V. S. Pritchett, New Statesman

There are perhaps ten active English-language writers whose
books I make haste to read as soon as possible... Norman Lewis
is one of them.
J. W. Lambert, Sunday Times

Previously published by

ELAND BOOKS

A VISIT TO DON OTAVIO

This book can be recommended as vastly enjoyable. Here is a book radiant with comedy and colour.
Raymond Mortimer, Sunday Times

Perceptive, lively, aware of the significance of trifles, and a fine writer. Applied to a beautiful, various, and still inscrutable country, these talents yield a singularly delightful result.
The Times

Mrs Bedford combines some of the qualities of Madame de Sévigné and of Brillat-Savarin, yet uniquely herself.
John Davenport, New Statesman

This book has that ageless quality which is what most people mean when they describe a book as classical. From the moment that the train leaves New York... it is certain that this journey will be rewarding. When one finally leaves Mrs Bedford on the point of departure, it is with the double regret of leaving Mexico and her company, and one cannot say more than that.
Elizabeth Jane Howard

Malicious, friendly, entertaining and witty.
Evening Standard

FROM REVIEWS OF OTHER BOOKS BY SYBILLE BEDFORD

She has a powerful and original intelligence - *Rebecca West*

A new writer of remarkable accomplishment - *Evelyn Waugh*

She has a great literary talent - *William Cooper*

She is a writer of extraordinary power - *Christopher Sykes*

This excellent writer - *Isaiah Berlin*